DESIGNING QUILTS

The Value of Value

By

Suzanne Tessier Hammond

Dedication

To Ellen Foster, for sharing her inner strength and determination.

Acknowledgments

Special thanks are extended to the following, for graciously sharing their quilts to be photographed:

Marilyn Anderson, Margo Barnreiter, Beverly Bell, Steven and Lydia Allen Berry, Ola Bouknight, Judy Goozée, Mary Ann Hatfield, Vivian Heiner, Bette Kassuba, Linda Levinson, Betty Oves, Reynola Pakusich, and Patricia Verd.

My sincere thanks also go to:

All my students who shared their excitement, enthusiasm, and results with me.

My fellow members of Quilters on the Edge, Joan Colvin, Hazel Ayre Hynds, Nell Clinton Moynihan, Betty Oves, and Kim Radder, for lighting the fire and keeping it going with their constant encouragement and support.

My friends in the Over the Quilt Gang, for all their help in decision making and for being an important part of my life for the past ten years.

Hazel Montague and Edeltraut Dow, for putting me ahead of everyone else in order to get my quilts finished in time.

Gene Carley, my personal smithy, for still taking the time out of his busy schedule to make my finger guards for me. I couldn't hand quilt without one.

Louis Myers, my friend and computer person, for putting it all together for me.

Ursula Reikes of That Patchwork Place, for patiently answering my many questions.

My family, for putting up with me during this difficult "birth."

And a very special thanks to Roberta Horton, for teaching me to appreciate all fabrics.

Credits

Editor-in-Chief . . . . Barbara Weiland
Technical Editor . . . . .Ursula Reikes
Managing Editor . . . . .Greg Sharp
Copy Editor .Sharon Rose
Proofreaders . . . . Tina Cook
Leslie Phillips
Text Designer . . . . Kay Green
Typesetter . . . . Shean Bemis
Photographer . . . . .Brent Kane
Illustrator . . . . John Paramore
Cover Designer . . . . Darcy Sinclair

Designing Quilts: The Value of Value ©
© 1994 by Suzanne Tessier Hammond

That Patchwork Place, Inc.
PO Box 118
Bothell, WA 98041-0118
USA

Printed in Hong Kong
99 98 97 96 95 94   6 5 4 3 2 1

**That Patchwork Place
Mission Statement**

We are dedicated to providing quality products that encourage creativity and promote self-esteem in our customers and our employees.

We strive to make a difference in the lives we touch.

That Patchwork Place is an employee-owned, financially secure company.

Hammond, Suzanne Tessier.
    Designing quilts : the value of value / Suzanne Tessier Hammond.
        p. cm.
    ISBN 1-56477-064-8 :
    1. Patchwork—Patterns. 2. Quilting—Patterns.
    3. Color in textile crafts.
    I. Title.
    TT835.H3353 1994
    746.46—dc20   94-18422
                                                        CIP

Contents

Preface

My love affair with fabric started many years ago when I was a teenager just out of high school. It all began innocently enough with the leftovers from four years' worth of clothing projects. Totally ignorant of what I was doing, I cut all the scraps into 4" squares and randomly sewed them together until I had enough to cover my bed.

Viewing all the fabrics together was a new experience. These leftover pieces were interacting! The combinations of colors, designs, values, and scales created visual texture and excitement. Each fabric had something to say now that there was competition.

When quiltmaking experienced its current revival, I took many quilting classes, covering a wide variety of subjects. As a result of my experimentation, I produced some beautiful quilts, but still only whispers emerged from my fabrics. Why was this happening? Why couldn't I evoke more power?

Looking back at that very first quilt and remembering how I reacted to it, I came to the conclusion that its simplicity was the very reason so many fabrics worked together successfully. My Amish and scrap quilts conveyed the same message—simplicity of pattern and design.

I also found that I experienced the most growth when I created a number of pieces on one theme. Each piece led to another. These observations helped me determine the elements on which to focus. I decided that perhaps by limiting myself to the barest essentials but working in a progression, I could achieve a better understanding of what was happening.

I searched for a simple block pattern that would show off my fabrics but could also offer a variety of design possibilities. I found it, and using it repeatedly allowed me to become familiar with the properties of the block and observe how they reacted to change. Furthermore, since my objective was to successfully use as many fabrics as possible in one quilt, I chose to focus on value rather than color in order to extend my fabric palette. What an eventful decision! What I learned about value is what this book is all about.

And so, with my elements chosen, my journey began. In the excitement along the way, I shared my results with others. I used my simple block to teach workshops on designing with value. Quilting friends and students all felt that this freedom and excitement should be shared, that everyone should have the opportunity to learn how to make their fabrics speak for them. This book is my invitation to you to join me on my journey.

Introduction

What is value? It is merely what our eyes perceive when reading how dark or light a color appears. If the definition is so simple, why then is it so difficult to identify? The reason is that our visual impressions of both color and value change once a piece is no longer alone. The final decision depends on what surrounds each piece. This simple truth—that a fabric must be viewed in a relationship—leads us to the realization that value is a major design element.

The information in this book will act as your guide in unraveling the mysteries of this element. Step by step, I will lead you to an understanding of value and its properties, including ways to make identification easier, how to "listen" to your fabrics, and suggestions for color sources. Once you understand these initial steps, you will learn how to use "my block," a traditional patchwork block.

I suggest you read through all the chapters before you begin playing with the quilt layouts in this book. This will prove helpful when making your fabric selections.

In working through the designs, you will begin to understand the true value of value in quilt design. You will find, as a result of your explorations, that even more design possibilities exist beyond those covered here. If you come across one of these detours along the way—go for it! That is how I developed all the designs in this book. Allow yourself the same freedom and you will be amazed with your results.

The Beginning

It was in Roberta Horton's classes that I learned about the fickleness of value and color and about how they perform their chameleon acts depending on their surroundings. The desire to learn more about these properties and how to make them work to my advantage started me on this adventure. Roberta took me through the crawling stage; then it was up to me to learn how to walk. My first step was to choose a quilt-block pattern for my experimentation with value. This would be my constant throughout the series. I kept the requirements to a minimum. The pattern had to be simple to draft, easy to construct, and made up of more than two pieces to allow enough areas for value placement. After all, my goal throughout the series was to explore design possibilities using a simple design but a complex palette. Having more than two pieces meant I could use more fabrics and thus enlarge my design choices. The Shaded Four Patch block I chose fit all three requirements.

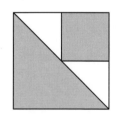

Shaded Four Patch Block

As my work progressed, each design that developed was another step in my journey. With each piece, I gained a deeper understanding of what I was doing, and more important, why I was doing it. Before long, ideas were pouring out of my head faster than I could write them down. I still have not exhausted all the possibilities.

Understanding Value

Light blocks

Dark blocks

Value is simply the darkness or lightness of a color. Color may enhance a quilt, but value establishes and solidifies the design. The degree of contrast between fabrics is what makes the design appear. Whether you are working with prints or solids, a limited or multiple color scheme, or specialty fabrics, the whole impact of the design can be lost if the value proportions are not balanced.

The design covers the largest area of the quilt's surface. If you are making a light quilt, the design area will contain predominantly light fabrics. For a dark quilt, you will substitute mostly dark fabrics in the same positions.

Dealing with fabrics strictly as light, medium, or dark eliminates some of the confusion and decision making involved when the element of color is added. Introducing a color scheme as one of your design elements limits your choice of fabrics since you are using only selected colors.

Now that you know the importance value plays in design, you can see why I felt my initial urge to explore it so thoroughly. The next step is to learn how to identify values and use them in the proper proportions.

I have already mentioned how fickle value can be. A medium fabric, for instance, can be dark or light, depending on what other values surround it.

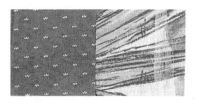

Dark   Light

Dark   Light

How can you achieve the right proportions when dealing with a large number of fabrics? If fabrics can change value merely by what surrounds them, how do you control all those fabrics without knowing their final placement beforehand?

First, establish some value categories. Most simple quilt patterns can be constructed using just dark and light fabrics. A medium value can be added to heighten or tone down the contrast between the other two values. This gives us the three basic value categories—dark, medium, and light.

That may be all you need to know when you are using a limited palette, but it is not broken down into enough categories for multicolor quilts. Since you do not know the final placement, you need to have a more definite answer to what value a fabric "reads" before combining it with others.

In order to provide reliable guidelines, I have developed five categories instead of just the original three. Following is a description of each, along with the part they play in designing.

Deep dark: Dark colors recede; they create depth in a design. If you use too much of this value, it creates the opposite effect—not enough depth. The design can become static or overpowering.

Medium dark: Use this value to break up the overpowering deep darks. Using more fabrics in the medium-dark value produces a softer, calmer effect.

Medium: This value plays one of the most important roles in designing. It is used to smooth the transition from light to dark so the change is not too disruptive to the eye. I also use this value to blur edges or tone down contrasts so the design doesn't stand out quite as much. This value creates restful areas when a quilt becomes too busy or bright.

Medium light: Use this value to offset the brightness created by the clear lights. Since I prefer darker quilts with a lower contrast, I use more medium lights than clear lights.

Clear light: Light values come toward you and appear larger. Clear light values come in handy when I want to make a medium fabric read dark. They can also be used to create areas of luminosity, where spaces on the surface of the quilt look as though they have a light behind them.

Keeping this information in mind, the next step is to determine in which category each fabric belongs. Some will be more obvious than others. You will find that quite a number of your fabrics will read the same value. That is because you probably tend to purchase the same types of fabrics over and over again since they are visually pleasing to you. You may need to supplement your palette if you find you don't have enough of some value categories.

How do you determine how many fabrics you will need in each value? In order to attain a pleasing balance, I devised this formula for myself:

For every one hundred blocks, select approximately

20 deep darks	15 medium lights
30 medium darks	10 clear lights
25 mediums	

It may be hard at first to distinguish one category from another without assistance. In the section on "Value-Determining Tools," beginning on page 11, I will introduce the tools and methods I use to help me determine value.

After you have chosen all your fabrics and determined in which of the five categories they belong, combine the five categories back into the original three—dark, medium, and light. Combine deep darks and medium darks to form the dark pile, keep the mediums the way they are, and combine medium lights and clear lights in the light pile.

Fabric Selection

My love of fabric is the reason I am a quiltmaker, and the variety in my collection reflects this. My fabrics date from the late 1800s to the present and include quite a selection from other countries. I have been sewing since I was fourteen, so I have had time to accumulate my treasures. As an artist, I consider myself a fabric "investor." Just like a painter, I need a well-rounded palette in order to make my picture. Keep that in mind as you start collecting fabric.

When making fabric selections, focus mainly on getting the right proportions of value. The only reason to mention color at this time is to remind you that you will be working with the entire color wheel. Your palette will consist of all colors in all values, with some represented more than others. Don't limit yourself to choosing your favorite colors. That will come later.

The other important thing to look for is variety in design scale. Different designs create different visual textures. Too much of one pattern can make a quilt look either too boring or too restless, too soothing or too overpowering. Scale can make or break the interest in a quilt. It plays the same role that high contrast does when dealing with value.

Since part of my challenge is making prints work together, I eliminated solids from my palette. Pin dots, small or low-contrast prints and geometrics can give the same effect since they all read as solids when viewed from a distance so I try to limit these too.

Large multicolor prints add a lot of movement, although too many next to each other can make an area too busy. You can calm an area down by replacing a few large prints with small prints. A subtle stripe or a small on-grain

Tip

If you cut a plaid or stripe off grain, it loses its orderliness and becomes busy. The same thing happens when you cut into a large multicolor print. Use small prints to calm a particular area. Reverse the formula to liven up a combination of small prints.

plaid will produce the same effect. The linear orderliness of the stripe or plaid offsets the circular movement of a large print.

In order to complete my scale palette, I look for a variety of designs in different sizes. I try to include as many as I can in each quilt to convey the feelings I want to express. Keep your eyes open for:

Small-scale prints

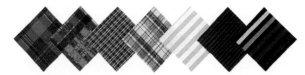

Large-scale prints

Dots: pin dot to quarter-size dot

Plaids and stripes: all sizes, both two-color and multicolor

Geometrics

Paisleys and swirls

Whimsical prints: anything from animals to wagon wheels. They can really add interest, especially if the motifs relate to the theme of the quilt.

Hawaiian

African

Japanese

Guatemalan

International fabrics from other countries, or those designed to look like they are from another culture.

You are now ready to begin selecting your fabrics. Include as many different fabrics as you can. Look in your scrap box for other choices. A 5" square is large enough to make even the largest piece in my block. If you feel that you do not have enough variety in your own fabric collection to fill all the value and scale requirements, try trading with other quilters.

The Design Wall

After you construct your blocks, you are ready to begin "playing on the wall." Having a design wall is an absolute necessity. You need to be able to step back from your work to truly see the design emerge. Laying your blocks on the bed or floor is not advantageous because you cannot look at your design directly. Viewing at an angle distorts the flow of the image. You will need a convenient location where you can leave your work in progress without having to put it away between design sessions. This affords the added advantage of having your work always on display. Each time you walk past it, a different element in the design will catch your eye. You will notice the trouble spots more easily because you won't be intentionally looking for them.

My design wall consists of a 4' x 8' sheet of lightweight acoustic ceiling material covered with white felt and mounted on a wall in my studio. When I'm working on a design, I pin a piece of fleece on top of the white felt attached to my design wall. I mark the fleece with a 4½" grid, using a permanent marking pen. One side is marked with a straight grid for straight sets, and the other is marked in a diagonal grid for diagonal sets.

This makes it easier to keep my designs in straight rows as I work, and I can keep track of where I am by matching the squares on my gridded wall with the corresponding ones on the paper layout I do of my quilt.

If you don't have room for a permanent design wall, make a portable one. All you need is a flat, even surface. Removing pictures from the wall temporarily may give you enough space to pin up a piece of fleece. Use a few straight pins to hold it up—the holes will not be noticeable when you replace the pictures.

If you need to remove your design wall for a period of time and do not want to disturb the design in progress, you can save your design using the following method. Leave your work on the fleece and pin a few sheets of tissue paper over the surface of the fleece. Starting from the bottom, roll the fleece over a long cardboard tube. When you reach the top, unpin the fleece from the wall and use a few pins to prevent it from unrolling. This is also a great way to transport designs in progress if the need arises.

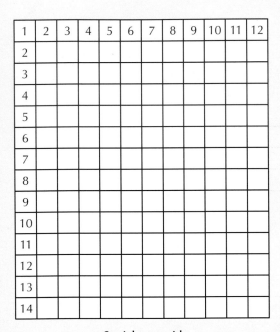

Straight set grid

Diagonal set grid

Value-Determining Tools

There are a number of tools on the market and items that you may already have at home that can help in determining value in your fabrics. Some are better for closeup work; others give a more distant view. I will point out the advantages and disadvantages of each so that you can choose the tools that will best serve your purposes and also fit your budget and time schedule.

Photocopying

Photocopying is one of the best methods of identifying value in individual fabrics because it produces a black-and-white image of your fabrics. Since color is no longer a factor, you get a better idea of what value they read.

I find this method quite helpful in determining the value of multicolor prints that contain equal amounts of several different colors. These prints never seem to read any definite value by themselves. I solved this dilemma by cutting strips of print fabrics and mixing them randomly with some strips of obvious dark and light fabrics. I taped the fabrics to a piece of paper and made a photocopy. Looking at the fabric in black and white gave me a better idea of where I can use these fabrics.

Remember, the goal is to be able to use all fabrics together. If you eliminate these seemingly valueless prints, you are eliminating not only a part of your palette but a part of the challenge as well.

Transparent Red Plastic

You can also view fabrics through a piece of transparent red plastic to determine their value. Place strips or squares of fabric side by side and view through the red plastic. The image is not as strong as a black-and-white image from a photocopier, but the colors are eliminated so that you can see the value of each fabric in relation to the others.

Reducing Glass

This tool is the opposite of a magnifying glass. It allows you to locate trouble spots by getting you visually farther away from your work, though physically you step back only a short distance. Its effect is similar to that of transparent red plastic, only here it is the illusion of distance at work, rather than the absence of color.

Tip

Reds and yellows tend to fade out when viewed through the red plastic. If you are planning to use a lot of these colors in a project, use one of the other methods to determine value.

Color photo of design

Photocopy of above color photo

Tip

You can tie a long, narrow ribbon around the cylinder of your peephole and hang it around your neck. It will always be there when you need it.

Camera

Looking through your camera lens is similar to looking at an object through a reducing glass. When you look through a camera lens, one eye is closed and the remaining eye sees only what is in the view of the lens. Your peripheral vision is cut off, so your eye can concentrate only on what is in front of it.

Another way to use your camera is to take pictures of your work as you make changes. A Polaroid camera is handy for this purpose. Black-and-white photos give the best results, but color pictures also work. Black-and-white photos have the added advantage of eliminating colors. (Make a photocopy of the color photograph to achieve the same results.)

Again, this works because the image is reduced so you can no longer easily pick out each individual fabric. The fabrics' values and the design they create when combined are most visible. It is easy to pick out the clustered areas of light and dark.

Binoculars

Many artists use binoculars "backwards" (looking through the reverse end) to determine value. Regular binoculars may be too high powered and make the image much too small; they can also be quite costly. I have found that the inexpensive toy models work best.

Peephole

If you want to get even farther away from your work than a reducing glass permits but not quite as far away as a pair of high-powered binoculars puts you, purchase a door peephole. Any hardware store should have them for under $5.00.

Use this little tool the same way you use the binoculars. Look through the end of the peephole to put distance between you and your design wall. (See page 11.) It is small and can fit into a pocket or sewing kit.

Mirror

Another tool I use is a full-length mirror that hangs on the back of my studio door opposite my design wall. Sometimes I get so engrossed in a design that I come to a complete halt. I don't know what to do next. My eye senses there is something wrong in the design, but I just can't seem to figure out what it is. Realizing that I have been working for too long from the same perspective, I know I need to look at the design from a new angle—with a different eye, so to speak. That is when I close my door and look at the design in the mirror with my back to the design wall. Because everything is reversed, I get the new view I need and I can usually remedy whatever is bothering me.

All of these tools can help you to determine the value of your fabrics and what combinations they produce. Any one of them can make your task easier. Try them out and choose the one that best meets your needs. Do try to have at least three or four of them on hand. You will find that different ones help during different stages of your work.

The Basic Block

The Shaded Four Patch block is so called to distinguish it from the regular Four Patch block. They are both made from the same number of templates. What makes them different?

The regular Four Patch is symmetrical and composed of four equal squares. The Shaded Four Patch, on the other hand, is not symmetrical. Splitting the same area in half diagonally first, then breaking up one of the resulting large triangles into a square and two equal half-square triangles results in asymmetrical corners.

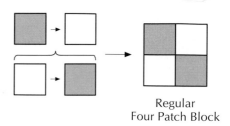

Regular
Four Patch Block

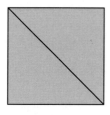 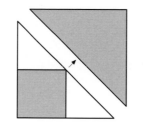 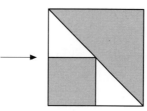

Shaded Four Patch Block

This allows for more design possibilities. In the rest of the text, I will refer to the Shaded Four Patch block as "my block."

I chose this block because of its simplicity. Because of their size and shape, the templates are easy to cut using the Template-Free® method. This method can be used whether you are cutting strips from yardage or squares from scraps. The block consists of a large 4½" half-square triangle, and a 2½" square in the same value, and two small 2½" half-square triangles of the opposite value. (See page 14 for full-size templates.) These are sewn together to make a 4" finished block. The large triangle is just the right proportion to show off your fabrics, especially large-scale prints.

Most of the quilt designs in this book only require eighty finished blocks. Begin by constructing 100 "practice" blocks. The extra twenty blocks will give you flexibility as you work on designs. Use these blocks to experiment with value and create some of the layouts in this book on your design wall.

Cutting

The triangles used to make this block are called half-square triangles. These triangles are half of a square with the short sides on the straight grain of the fabric and the long side on the bias.

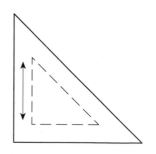

Template-Free Method

To cut both the large and small half-square triangles using the Template-Free method, cut strips from your fabric using a rotary cutter and ruler.

At this point, your fabrics are in three piles—light, medium, and dark.

1. Using a rotary cutter and ruler, cut a 4⅞"-wide and a 2½"-wide strip from the width of each fabric in the dark value pile if you are making dark blocks, or from the light and medium value piles if you are making light blocks.

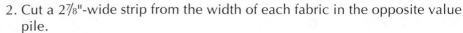

2. Cut a 2⅞"-wide strip from the width of each fabric in the opposite value pile.

3. Cut each strip into 3 equal lengths (approximately 15"). Keep 1 piece and save the other 2 pieces for future projects or use them as trading pieces to fill in your palette. Return all strips to their proper value piles.

4. Align a number of same-width strips on top of each other and cut them into the appropriate-size squares. From the 4⅞" strips, cut 4⅞" squares; from the 2⅞" strips, cut 2⅞" squares; from the 2½" strips, cut 2½" squares.

5. Cut the 4⅞" and 2⅞" squares once diagonally to yield half-square triangles.

Remember that each square yields 2 triangles; divide the number of triangles you need by 2. This will give you the number of squares you need. Example: 100 triangles divided by 2 = 50 squares.

Note: Do not cut 2½" squares diagonally. Each block requires 1 square.

You can also use your rotary cutter and ruler to cut triangles and squares out of scraps. Skip the strip-cutting step and go directly to cutting squares. Cut the scraps into the appropriate-size squares (step 4) and proceed as before with the diagonal cut from corner to corner (step 5).

With striped fabrics or special prints, the direction of the stripe or print takes precedence over the direction of the grain. If they are not cut on grain, they are less stable and will stretch, so it is important to handle them carefully. If you plan to use these pieces along the outside edges of the quilt, staystitch ⅛" from the raw edge to avoid stretching.

Template Method

Circumstances will arise when you must cut pieces individually, such as when you want to cut out a specific area in your fabric. Trace the templates onto plastic template material and cut them out. If there is a color, theme, or design you want to feature, center the template over the desired area and cut out that piece. If the piece is not cut on grain, take care when handling it to avoid stretching.

Tip

If you use more than one measuring tool for the different shapes, make sure that all the tools are made by the same company. This ensures accurate measurements.

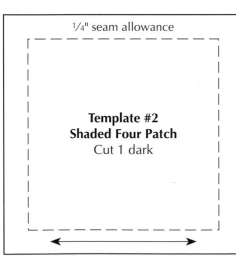

¼" seam allowance

Template #2
Shaded Four Patch
Cut 1 dark

Template #3
Shaded Four Patch
Cut 2 light

Template #1
Shaded Four Patch
Cut 1 dark

straight of grain

Assembling the Block

There is one last step before you begin sewing the block pieces together. You need to merge your three value piles of light, medium, and dark into two value piles by combining the lights and mediums into one stack. Mix the fabrics well within each stack to get a true random effect.

As you assemble the blocks, sew pieces together as they come off their respective stacks. No matching is allowed unless a project calls for it. The finished block will always be a surprise.

Follow the piecing diagrams, using chain-piecing techniques (page 58) to piece the blocks.

1. Sew a small light triangle to one side of a dark square.

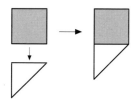

2. Sew a second small light triangle to the square as shown. Press the seam allowances toward the darker fabric. Be careful to avoid stretching the bias edges.

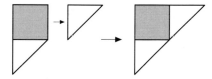

3. Sew the pieced triangle to a large dark triangle to complete the block.

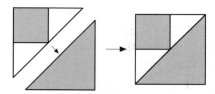

Note: Repeat with opposite values for a predominantly light block. Don't agonize over the combinations of fabrics. What you are seeing up close as a block of four mismatched fabrics will blend with all the other blocks, until all you see is the design created by the values you have chosen.

4. Measure each block to make sure that all blocks are the same size. Use a Bias Square® ruler to trim each block to a uniform size. Some blocks may be off by only a few threads, others by as much as 1/8". Remember to trim from all four sides or your block will be lopsided. If you want your quilt to lie flat and hang straight with even edges, this step is very important.

Quilt Layouts

The design layouts provided on pages 64–77 are only a few of the designs that resulted from my experimentation. Use your practice blocks to duplicate, learn from, and modify my layouts. Following the guidelines below, use the value-determining tools on pages 11–12 to assist you in arranging the blocks in a pleasing manner.

When I began playing with my blocks on the design wall, I placed them all facing one direction when creating each new design. I call these "single" designs.

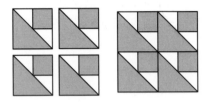

Single Design

I found each value formed a more solid line when I rotated every other block 180°. I refer to these as "double" designs.

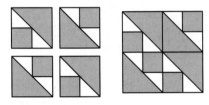

Double Design

Each version of a design results in a totally different-looking quilt. When you begin, try both the single and double versions of each design as shown in the layouts. This way, you can actually see how value can be manipulated for the desired effect. Step back and view your design as it forms. Use your value-determining tools to aid you along the way.

As you work your way through the layouts, you will notice that each design leads to the next one. This is all due to a few rotations of the block. Each rotation provides new design options to pursue.

I produced the block repeat layouts on pages 76–77 by using a small number of blocks to create a larger design element. Repeated side by side, the larger design elements produce a wonderful secondary design.

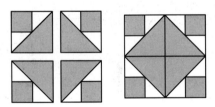

Block Repeat

You can add a narrow sashing between the larger design elements to create completely different designs.

You will find that some designs do not stand out as well as others. That may be because you are using a random multi-fabric palette. If the design looks blurry or seems too busy, it is telling you that it needs a more controlled combination of fabrics or some other element of continuity. Don't discount these designs. Try them later, using a more limited color scheme of two or three colors (controlled) or special fabrics (continuity).

Go back to the five value categories on page 7. Photocopy the information and pin it to the side of your design wall so it is always handy for reference. Reacquaint yourself with each category and its various properties—what role it plays in creating the design.

If the design disappears in a certain area, use your value categories to correct the problem. Substitute a few low-contrast blocks with blocks higher in contrast, and the design reappears. Do not replace all of the low-contrast blocks—just a few bold substitutes will carry the design through. Use the low-contrast blocks you removed to tone down another area that is too busy.

Whether you like dark or light fabric, you will see that either one can make a stunning quilt. Feel free to substitute your own theme or color recipe in any of the projects as well as to change the design value from dark to light if you prefer. Just reverse the value positions in the fabric requirements. You can also add dimension by combining blocks from both values in one quilt. (See Octopus's Garden below.) The use of many large-print fabrics and the diagonal setting create movement. Fabrics featuring marine life and the fish quilting design further support the theme.

Most of the layouts use a straight-set design. Designs can also be set symmetrically with each half a mirror image of the other, or the designs can be offset.

Setting the blocks on point reveals still other design possibilities. Layouts 3, 4, 15, and 17 are examples of designs where the blocks are set on point.

Mirror image

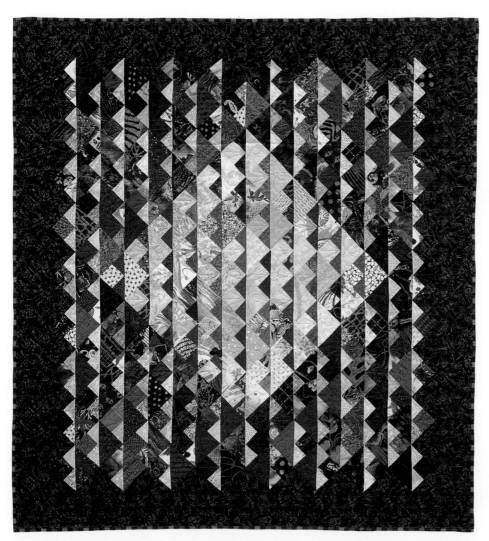

Offset

Octopus's Garden
by Suzanne T. Hammond, 1993, Bellingham, Washington, 54¼" x 59½". Hand quilted by Hazel Montague. (Variation of Layout #3) (Directions begin on page 48.)

Take a photograph of each new design as it develops and draft it on graph paper. Pictures provide you with your own gallery of quilts to use as a reference guide and also serve to document your growth—a growth I guarantee will occur with each new attempt.

The layouts are easy to follow, no matter what value you choose to use as your focus. Just follow the placement of the blocks in the diagram. If a block is placed in the wrong direction, you will notice it immediately when you step back and view it, using one of your value-determining tools.

The single and double ladder layouts below have been shaded to show you the different results you can achieve when you reverse the values.

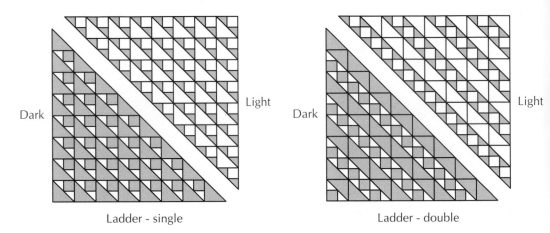

Dark   Light   Dark   Light

Ladder - single   Ladder - double

I hope by now you can see that your options are endless. As you work through the different layouts, you will start to recognize some of these options. As you get more confident, experiment by combining design elements from two or three layouts and see what develops.

Combination of several layouts

When you have found the design you want to use for your quilt, you can either use your practice blocks, or you can make new blocks in a more controlled palette. The blocks you have already made will not be wasted. Keep using them to create new ideas for designs.

Every time I teach a value workshop, there are always some students who arrive believing you need a color scheme in order to make a quilt. I quickly inform them that, in this class, color is a "four-letter word." Our only objective at this point is to focus on value using every color on the color wheel. Once you understand how to create designs based on value, you will be one step closer to understanding how to work with colors effectively.

During the design stage, we discuss using certain colors to liven up dull or uninteresting areas in a quilt. Bits of yellow scattered throughout a mostly dark quilt can really liven it up. Red adds a sparkle to a boring scrap quilt. These are called accent colors.

Used sparingly, an accent color stands out among the others. A small amount strewn across the quilt's surface is all that is needed to add interest. Just about any color can achieve the same effect. Again, it is all relative to the surrounding fabrics. You don't have to be a color expert to know how to use color successfully.

Probably the best place to look for inspiration is right in your own fabric collection. Look at your multicolor fabrics, including prints and plaids.

Look at those that have three or more colors in them. Notice which color is the strongest and how much of it appears in the print. Do the same with the rest of the colors. What values do they read? How much is there of each color, each value? Is there an accent color? These are all important clues. You can plan a whole quilt using this method. Remember, the key to putting it all together successfully is proportion.

Other ideas for color schemes come from pictures and ads in magazines or photos of decorating schemes and garden layouts found in indoor/outdoor periodicals. Large corporations tend to use a lot of color in their promotional literature. The subject matter is not important—only that it is visually pleasing to you.

Try some of these suggestions. I am confident they will work as well for you as they do for me. You may be surprised when you realize how much inspirational material has been right there all along.

Color in prints

Look for color schemes that convey a certain mood or emotion. Try to repeat that same mood or feeling using fabric. Experiment with different values of each color until that feeling emerges. Keep referring to your color picture to guide your decision making.

Adding a Second Block

I first combined two different blocks during an exercise with my study group. Our goal was to find two patterns that, when placed next to each other, would form a new design. Unfortunately, both the original blocks and the new pattern that evolved were quite complex to piece.

Then I wondered what would happen if I tried the same exercise using my block. Let's explore the possibilities together. Since my objective is simplicity, the second block should be no more complex than the original block and should not overshadow the original block. Repeating one of the shapes in my block is a place to begin.

Shaded Four Patch Block

A simple repeat of the 2" square yields a Four Patch block equal in size to my finished block.

Joining two of the large half-square triangles to form a square produces another block that also shows possibilities.

Regular Four Patch Block

Half-Square Triangle Block

Since both these blocks are simple in form, they should enhance and work well with my block, rather than detract from it.

The Four Patch block provides more value-placement opportunities than the half-square triangle block, so this is the first block we'll combine with my original block.

Beginning with the single ladder layout, alternate my block with the Four Patch block, starting each new row with a different block.

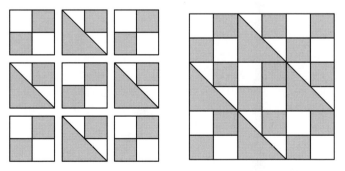

Single Ladder with Four Patch Block

Each shape chains nicely as it forms dark and light diagonal lines. The second layout, the double ladder, looks even more interesting.

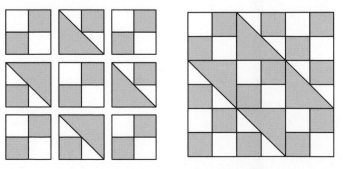

Double Ladder with Four Patch Block

A more effective design is emerging—but why? The 4" half-square triangle in my block occupies the most prominent value position in all the designs because it is so much bigger than the other pieces. By reversing the units so that the half-square triangles face each other, the value is concentrated in rows rather than being distributed over the quilt's surface.

In making my "Scrap Ladder" quilt, below, I used Four Patch blocks with medium to high contrast. Randomly composed Shaded Four Patch blocks alternate with randomly pieced Four Patch blocks in this multi-fabric quilt. No color recipe was used, but the various reds scattered throughout the design help tie all the colors together.

Scrap Ladder
by Suzanne T. Hammond, 1988,
Bellingham, Washington,
45" x 61". (Layout #20)

Tribute to Suzanne *by Betty Oves, 1993,*
Bellingham, Washington, 52½" x 68½". (Layout #20)
(Directions begin on page 52.)

Detail of **Tribute**
to Suzanne,
shown above.

"Tribute to Suzanne," also a scrap ladder quilt using a Four Patch block, has an even stronger diagonal pattern.

The second quilt reads like a "richer cousin" of the first, all due to a few changes in design elements. What created the greatest change was toning down the contrast in the Four Patch blocks between the diagonal rows of light and dark. Reds and bright fabrics add life and sparkle to offset the many deep, dark fabrics.

The light diagonal rows were formed using high-contrast Four Patch blocks, while muddier, low-contrast blocks were used to create the darker rows. As you can see, you can create different results by regulating the value placement.

Extending the rows into the border using the half-square triangle block enhances the quilt even further. The half-square triangle blocks are composed of the desired value in one triangle and the border fabric in the other triangle. Adding another 2" border of the same fabric makes the design appear to float on the surface area of the quilt and also frames the entire piece effectively.

Notice the bits of lime green and bright turquoise that were used as supporting accents for the major red accent. These scattered colors add sparkle to the quilt, as if someone had sprinkled it with confetti.

With these ideas in mind, continue examining the layouts and look for new ideas. See what happens when a combination of all three units is used. Who would ever imagine that such simplicity could offer so many possibilities? It is definitely worth exploring.

My own experimentation led me to the conclusion that adding a second block can serve an even more important purpose. Sometimes it can be used to control a "negative" space created by the design; however, this background area should support the main design, not compete with it. The bird and flower designs on pages 76–77 are fine examples of this. Following are a few other examples of how a second block can solve design problems.

My first opportunity to try this concept was with "Nicole's Star."

When four Star blocks composed of just my block are placed next to each other, they form a busy pattern that completely overwhelms the star points.

The outer corners of the Star blocks need to be simplified in order to bring out the star design.

Substituting a Four Patch block in each corner does not simplify the design; again the star points are lost.

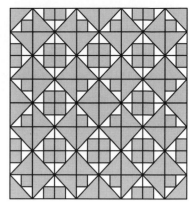

Shaded Four Patch
Corners

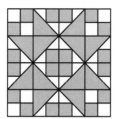

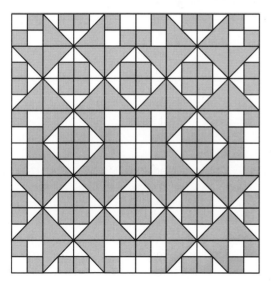

Four Patch Corners

Nicole's Star
by Suzanne T. Hammond, 1993, Bellingham, Washington, 78" x 110". In making a "freedom" quilt for her daughter's twenty-first birthday, Suzanne chose the star to symbolize her daughter's importance to her. Machine quilted by Edeltraut Dow. (Layout #30) (Directions begin on page 55.)

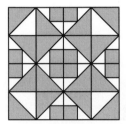

Plain Square Corners

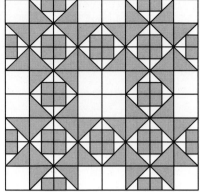

A plain square produces a rigid block formation, which is not what I wanted.

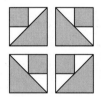

Half-Square
Triangle Corners

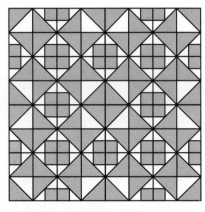

I finally reached a happy medium by using the half-square triangle block.

A new design forms where the Star blocks touch, surrounding and emphasizing the star shapes, yet allowing a smooth flow from one star to the other.

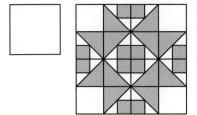

Arrow

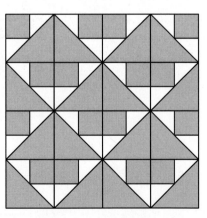

Side-by-Side Arrows

"Family Values" on page 26 posed a similar problem. This time I needed an area in which to appliqué the child. The design idea originated with the Arrows block repeat.

In viewing the design, you can see how alternating rows of arrows, now seen as huts, leave no place to appliqué the child.

By replacing my block with a half-square triangle block for the rooftops, I eliminated the alternating rows of huts. This made the appliquéd child more visible.

The concept "less is sometimes more" becomes evident when you need to create a calm design area.

Allowing myself to follow this detour—adding a second block—enriched my understanding of value. Restructuring the background opened new avenues to explore.

Replace top corners with half-square triangle blocks to calm the background area.

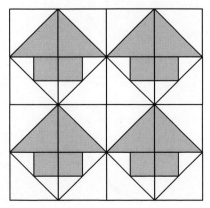

"Where Have All the Elephants Gone?" is a result of that exploration. The idea for this quilt evolved from an old apron I found at a garage sale. Majestic jungle animals were silk-screened around the edges of the apron. At home, as I looked at it more closely, I realized that the elephant was not represented—perhaps an omen predicting the slaughter of the breed for their ivory. Would it be possible to incorporate the images on the apron and this theme into an idea for a quilt?

Let's look at the options together. This way, you can get a better idea of how I approached this challenge. First, simplicity is always a major factor governing our design. Second, we want to use a multi-fabric palette. The new elements we need to consider are the dual focal points: the jungle animals and a design that can stand by itself without overpowering the first focal point.

Step one involves simplifying choices. Selecting a limited color scheme can create focus on the design area by providing continuity throughout the quilt surface. The colors on the apron are green, brown, and rust. Those three colors, in all values, will be the focus.

That was simple enough. The next step is to figure out a way to incorporate the animals, allowing them to share the spotlight without competing for it. In previous quilts, you saw how I added a second block to calm down an area. If we consider the animal panels as part of the background, a second block could be added to fill in the rest of the background without creating a distraction.

I cut out the animals, saving as much fabric as possible. This resulted in various-size pieces. Since my block can be divided into 2" increments, I trimmed the animal panels into sizes divisible by two and filled in empty spaces with 2" squares of low-contrast fabrics to form the completed blocks.

It was necessary to piece some of the panels to make them large enough, but the piecing is hardly noticeable. The blank square was pieced from what was left of the apron's center. The small 2" square containing part of the vegetation breaks up the emptiness of the blank square and draws your eye to the quilted "ghost" of the elephant.

I added the striped inner border to frame the background area. The plaid outer border then frames the entire quilt. Extending the design into the outer border allowed it to continue uninterrupted so it stands out even more. The emphasis on the bolder design acts as a frame to show off the animal panels. Each design element supports the other due to the careful use of value.

Look through pattern books and magazines for other simple blocks that could be auditioned for future design ideas. Sketch each new block on graph paper and try shading the design in different ways. Eliminate any ideas that don't immediately show promise. No sense wasting time when there are other patterns waiting to be tried!

Try out your new ideas with your already-constructed blocks, using your value-determining tools to help you along the way. Take pictures as each new design emerges. This will allow you to pick out the design elements you like best from each photo. Proceed with these parts to make a whole quilt.

This kind of experimentation allowed me to grow one step at a time. If you follow my lead, you too will achieve this growth and also a greater understanding of value and its value in designing quilts. You won't be disappointed.

Where Have All the Elephants Gone?
by Suzanne T. Hammond, 1993, Bellingham, Washington, 57" x 73".

Interpreting the Idea

My understanding of value did not come about overnight. Each new experiment brought me one step closer. The pictures in this book only show the results of my experiences. By sharing some of the thought processes involved in making these pieces, I hope to provide you with a better understanding of how I got from one point to the next.

In the layout section, I mentioned that you can make a design disappear or reappear just by replacing a few blocks with blocks of a different contrast (either high or low), depending on what is needed to make the design successful.

"Old-Fashioned Love" is a good example of how this works. Notice that the top points of some of the hearts read differently.

Some points are lighter than others, but since most read dark, they help the lighter value carry the design through uninterrupted. The borders support the scattered bits of red throughout the quilt to add continuity and give it that old-fashioned look.

Old-Fashioned Love
by Suzanne T. Hammond, 1993,
Bellingham, Washington, 50" x 54".
Machine quilted by Edeltraut Dow.
(Layout #27) (Directions begin on page 46.)

Family Values
by Suzanne T. Hammond, 1993,
Bellingham, Wahington, 40" x 40".
(Variation of Layout #21)

Sometimes you will want to "lose" the design—to purposely blur the edges. In the quilt "Family Values" (page 26), the child is the focal point. The inspiration for this piece came from the old African saying, reverse appliquéd at the bottom of the quilt, and the feud between Murphy Brown and then incumbent vice-president Dan Quayle, over what constitutes a family. The use of the African fabrics complements the theme's source and places further focus on the huts.

I chose a light value for the center background area to showcase the small silhouette. Progressing toward the edges of the quilt, I lowered the contrast between values to portray cool, shaded areas. This allowed the rondavels (huts) to remain visible but prevented them from overpowering the figure of the child.

I used this same idea to complete the borders for "Ivy Trellis." Careful control of values was necessary to successfully combine the two challenging elements in this quilt. I used only plaids and stripes to create the color gradation. The fickleness of value is evident as the color gradates across the surface. Even the lighter large tri-angles appear dark because of the lighter values that surround them.

Rather than box in the design with a simple frame border using one fabric, I was aiming for a more open feeling. I achieved this by repeating the block in the border, again using low-contrast blocks. Most of the border blocks are composed of grays and blacks, but some contain just a hint of the color they are near. This is called an "implied" border and, as you can see, it can be very effective.

Ivy Trellis
by Suzanne T. Hammond, 1991, Bellingham, Washington, 56" x 71". Machine quilted by Arlene Stafford. (Variation of Layout #8)

Cotton Candy Weave
by Suzanne T. Hammond, 1993,
Bellingham, Washington, 40½" x 40½".
(Layout #18) Directions begin on
page 44.

"Cotton Candy Weave" is a good example of how the most subtle change in value can improve a design. Proper placement of both value and color produced the weave design. The secondary pin-wheel design that results is an added bonus and a perfect place to feature family photos or a theme block. The color recipe is simply darker values of the colors that appear in the background fabric.

Now compare it with "A Tribute to Hoffman" and "Fl-air Weave."

In these two quilts, the weave design appears less prominent, more subdued. What was done to make each piece look so different? Let's evaluate each quilt and compare their elements.

The design area in all three quilts is formed with dark values, but "Cotton Candy Weave" differs from the other two in a number of ways.

A Tribute to Hoffman
by Bette Kassuba, 1993,
Woodinville, Washington,
40" x 40". (Layout #18)

- The background of "Cotton Candy Weave" is composed entirely of the same clear light fabric.
- It has a definite color scheme (the weave colors being darker versions of the three pastel colors in the background).
- The value of the small half-square triangle (in the position where the design lines intersect and change color) was changed from the background value to a medium value of the corresponding color. Different-scale fabrics were used—some large, some small, even plaids and dots.
- The surface floats on a border of the same clear background fabric, so the weave design really stands out.

The other two weave designs are closely related to each other, but they differ from each other as well. Both share some elements, such as the use of only large-scale prints. Both backgrounds were made using a variety of fabrics and, most important, a variety of values.

In "A Tribute to Hoffman," the artist used a large proportion of clear lights. Some of the bold Hoffman™ prints contain bits of those same clear lights. Between the two, they interact and make the surface sparkle like a color wash.

The background in "Fl-air Weave" has a higher proportion of medium values with just a small amount of clear lights distributed across the

Fl-air Weave by Reynola Pakusich, 1993, Bellingham, Washington, 48" x 60". *(Layout #18)*

quilt's surface. The large-scale airbrushed Fl-air™ fabrics are lower in contrast than the Hoffman fabrics. Many of the fabrics are deep darks, so the mediums help support them. Using too many clear lights would make those deep darks overpower the medium darks, and the weave design would no longer be apparent.

Since a random background was used, no attention was paid to changing the value of the small half-square triangle as I did in "Cotton Candy Weave." The weaves are interrupted, but the connection is still evident.

The final change appears in the borders. The decision by both artists to frame their designs, rather than float them as I did, was a much better choice for these quilts. The dark-value borders further support the design surface. They help contain the large-scale prints and at the same time produce the sparkle that is evident in both quilts.

In the section describing scale (pages 8–9), I mentioned that using many large-scale prints in one piece could be a real challenge due to all the interaction they produce. These two quilts are fine examples of how it can be done successfully.

Hawaii Review
by Suzanne T. Hammond,
1993, Bellingham, Washington,
34½" x 34½". (Layout #14)
(Directions begin on page 42.)

"Hawaii Review" was my first attempt to feature bold, high-contrast fabrics. I experimented one step at a time so that I could understand what was taking place.

This quilt contains very few deep darks and medium darks. Many of the fabrics actually read medium when they are alone. I chose a solid, clear light background so that these mediums, sprinkled with a few darks, carry the design lines through the entire quilt. If I had used a high-contrast print or a medium value for the background, the design would have been lost. Since there is very little dark value, the border doesn't have to be really dark to contain the design.

"A Bit of Africa" posed a similar problem. Like "Hawaii Review," the fabrics all read medium value. I again used a high-contrast background but chose to work in the opposite value to see what would happen.

A Bit of Africa
by Suzanne T. Hammond,
1992, Bellingham, Washington,
33" x 33". (Variation of Layout
#14) (Collection of Steven and
Lydia Allen Berry)

The deep dark fabric background was repeated in the border so the entire design floats on the surface and really comes forward.

At first glance, this quilt appears to read gold. Look carefully at each individual fabric and notice all the other colors that are included. These bits of scattered color add excitement to the design.

I played it safe with "Hawaii Review" and "A Bit of Africa." In order to feature the fabrics without competition, I chose high-contrast backgrounds.

"Japanese Lanterns" was an even bigger challenge. Again, the background fabric (the small triangles) is the same throughout so that it does not compete with the featured fabrics.

The difference is that there is much less contrast between the background and the featured fabrics. The background fabric consists of a small blue tone-on-tone linear print. This linear element helps calm down the large-scale prints, performing the same service that the high-contrast background does in the African quilt.

To emphasize the lantern shape, I made the large triangles that make up each lantern from the same fabric. The lanterns often disappear into the background and pop up again somewhere else. Again, there are spatters of other colors everywhere, even though the quilt reads as blue overall. The inky blue border enhances the color scheme and nicely contains the design area.

Look for these elements in the other photos throughout the book. Notice value, scale, and color proportions and how each affects the designs that are formed. Keep these thoughts in mind while designing your own quilts and you, too, will achieve a better understanding of what has taken place.

I have enjoyed every step of my experimentation, which has not come to an end with the publication of this book. I am still forging ahead in my series as I keep asking myself "What if?" with each new turn. Allow yourself the freedom to do the same and enjoy the design process.

Japanese Lanterns
by Suzanne T. Hammond, 1993,
Bellingham, Washington,
32" x 42". (Layout #22)

Gallery

Shared Memories *by Patricia S. Verd, 1993, Anacortes, Washington, 43" x 50". Recalling fond memories of her daughter as a little girl with her kitty, Patricia chose this preprinted panel as the ideal beginning for the quilt she wanted to make for her new granddaughter. The clear values used in the center help put extra focus on the panel. The "night sky," composed of many star-print fabrics, and the Heart block—all cat prints—are both good examples of fabrics supporting a theme. Machine quilted by Patsi Hanseth. (Variation of Layout #13) (Collection of Kaylee Michele Huie)*

Have a Heart by Beverly J. Bell, 1993, Bellingham, Washington, 80" x 92". Substituting some of the Shaded Four Patch blocks in the background with Four Patch blocks creates a calmer background. This change also strengthens the heart design. Machine quilted by Barbara Ford. (Variation of Layout #27)

Valued Leftovers by Linda Levinson, 1993, Mukilteo, Washington, 53" x 45". The soft palette, along with good control over value placement, makes this quilt seem to float on air. The center area, composed of mostly clear light blocks, is framed nicely by the surrounding row of medium blocks. Returning to the clear lights on the outermost edges produces the airy effect. Machine quilted by Patsi Hanseth. (Layout #11)

Antique Shaded Four Patch by Mary Hartley Ivers, c. 1900, 70" x 90". The Shaded Four Patch block has endured the test of time as evidenced by this turn-of-the-century quilt top. Even then, it was treasured as an ideal unit for scrap quilts. Hand pieced by Mary Hartley Ivers. (Layout #1) (Collection of author)

Potpourri *by Linda Levinson, 1993, Mukilteo, Washington, 53" x 53". Allowing the blocks to go into the border lets this design frame itself. The darker border acts as a backdrop to showcase the design surface. Machine quilted by Patsi Hanseth. (Layout #16)*

Value's Victorious Variety *by Margo Barnreiter, 1993, Bellingham, Washington, 41" x 56".*
Ample use of deep darks, broken up and accented by dark reds throughout the design area,
gives this quilt its jewel–like appearance. It combines parts from two different layouts. (Lay-
outs #6 and #8)

Bluebirds and Butterflies by Marilyn Anderson, 1993, Oak Harbor, Washington, 32" x 40". Combining three simple units leads to some interesting design possibilities. The butterflies are the maker's interpretation of the Lantern block, and the birds resulted from a few twists of the Heart block. (Layouts #22 and #29)

Waterlilies by Marilyn Anderson, 1993, Oak Harbor, Washington, 24" x 44". This is another fine example of combining three simple units together to create a new design. An offshoot of the Heart block, a few unit substitutions, and this wonderful flower appears. (Layout #28)

Stormy Weather by Suzanne T. Hammond, 1990, Bellingham, Washington, 35" x 35". This quilt was my first attempt at using nothing but plaids and stripes. I cut the fabrics on grain and somewhat matched the borders to produce a calm, orderly effect. (Layout #24)

1890s Revisited by Judy Goozee, 1993, Camano Island, Washington, 54" x 62". Using some favorite reproduction fabrics and a careful choice of value proportions makes this quilt a success. Fven distribution of a small amount of deep darks throughout the design surface prevents them from seeming to appear out of place. (Layout #14)

Black Iris by Ola Bouknight, 1993, Bellingham, Washington, 58" x 62". Combining the two featured fabrics—the Hoffman™ "Antique Medallions" and the Fl-air™ airbrushed panels—gives the quilt a look of simple elegance. The secondary color in the Hoffman fabric livens up the background without drawing the focus away from the iris panels. (Layout #1)

Four Patch I
by Vivian Heiner, 1993,
Seattle, Washington,
43" x 43". This overall
random design emerged
while "playing" with the
units. Notice the small
number of bright pink
blocks—just enough to add
some excitement.

Love Letters by Mary Ann Hatfield, 1993, Anacortes, Washington,
27" x 27". A controlled combination of scrap fabrics in these blocks, set
on point, creates this wonderful design. The introduction of the Hourglass
block as an alternate square allows the envelope shapes to become the focal
point. (Layout #26)

More Love Letters by Mary Ann Hatfield, 1993, Anacortes, Washington,
20" x 20". Limiting the color recipe to the traditional red-and-white color
scheme and selecting only heart-print fabrics gives this piece its "love" theme.
Varying the sizes of the heart motifs (variety of scale) keeps the envelopes from
blending into the background. (Layout #26)

The Quilts

Specific yardage requirements are not provided for the blocks in the following quilt plans. The projects call for a large assortment of fabrics in various color schemes. Use whatever fabric yardage or scraps you have on hand that fit into the color scheme. If you purchase yardage, fat quarters or fat eighths work well. You may have quite a bit of fabric left over if you are only cutting one or two pieces from each fabric. But remember, you can always use your leftovers for other projects. Yardage requirements and cutting instructions are based on 42" of usable fabric after preshrinking

The cutting section in each quilt plan lists the number of pieces to cut from the required fabrics. This will give you an idea of approximately how much fabric you need. Triangles and squares can be cut from various sizes of fabric. To quick-cut the large triangles, you will need pieces of fabric at least 5" x 5". Small triangles require at least 3" x 3", and small squares only need 2½" x 2½".

Hawaii Review

Quilt Stats

Quilt Size: 34½" x 34½"

Number of Blocks:
36 Shaded Four Patch

Design Layout:
Double Barn Raising
Layout #14

Design Value: Dark

Theme: Hawaiian

Color Scheme:
Blue, purple, and pink

Color photo on page 30.

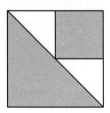

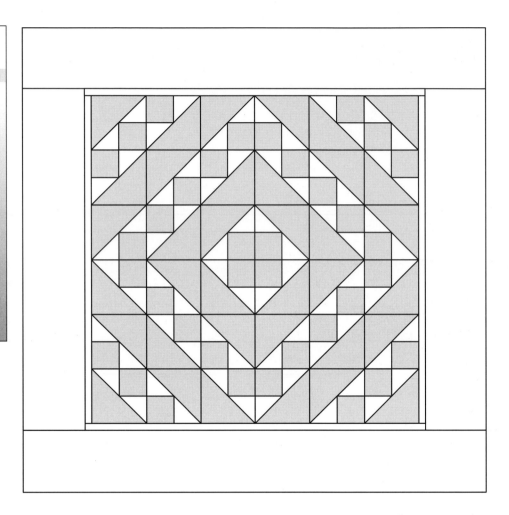

Materials: *44"-wide fabric*

Assorted dark and medium fabrics for blocks
⅓ yd. light background for blocks
¼ yd. for inner border
⅔ yd. for outer border
¼ yd. for binding
1¼ yds. for backing

Cutting

Follow directions on pages 13–14 for cutting triangles and squares.

From assorted darks and mediums, cut:
18 squares, each 4⅞" x 4⅞"; cut squares once diagonally to yield 36 half-
    square triangles **OR** cut 36 Template #1;
36 squares, each 2½" x 2½", **OR** cut 36 Template #2.

From light background, cut:
36 squares, each 2⅞" x 2⅞"; cut squares once diagonally to yield 72 half-
    square triangles **OR** cut 72 Template #3.

From inner border fabric, cut:
2 strips, each 1" x 24½", for sides;
2 strips, each 1" x 25½", for top and bottom.

From outer border fabric, cut:
2 strips, each 5" x 25½", for sides;
2 strips, each 5" x 34½", for top and bottom.

Directions

1. Follow the general directions on page 15 for assembling the Shaded Four
   Patch blocks.
2. Arrange the blocks into 6 rows of 6 blocks each as shown in the quilt plan
   at left.
3. Sew the blocks together into horizontal rows. Press the seams in opposite
   directions from row to row. Sew the rows together, making sure to match
   the seams between the blocks.
4. Sew the inner border strips to the sides first, then to the top and bottom
   edges of the quilt top, as shown on page 60. Add the outer border strips
   in the same manner.
5. Layer the quilt top with batting and backing; baste.
6. Quilt as desired.
7. Bind the edges of the quilt.

Cotton Candy Weave

Quilt Stats

Quilt Size: 40½" x 40½"

Number of Blocks:
72 Shaded Four Patch
9 plain center squares

Design Layout: Weave
Layout #18

Design Value: Dark

Color Scheme:
Purple, green, and pink

Color photo on page 28.

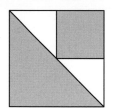

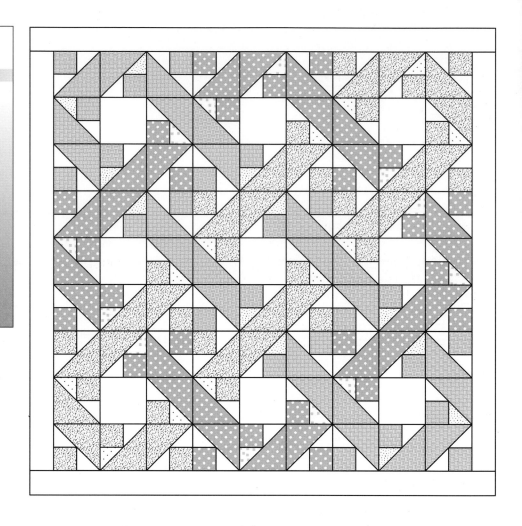

Color Key

▦	Dark greens	▦	Medium greens
▦	Dark purples	▦	Medium purples
▦	Dark pinks	▦	Medium pinks

Materials: *44"-wide fabric*

For blocks:
    12 different dark greens
    12 different dark purples
    12 different dark pinks
    6 different medium greens
    6 different medium purples
    6 different medium pinks
1 yd. light background for blocks and border
¼ yd. for binding
1⅓ yds. for backing

Cutting

Follow directions on pages 13–14 for cutting triangles and squares.

From *each* of the dark fabrics, cut:

1 square, 4⅞" x 4⅞"; cut squares once diagonally to yield 2 half-square
    triangles **OR** cut 2 Template #1 (total of 72 triangles);
2 squares, each 2½" x 2½", **OR** cut 2 Template #2, (total of 72 squares).

From *each* of the medium fabrics, cut:

1 square, 2⅞" x 2⅞"; cut squares once diagonally to yield 2 half-square
    triangles **OR** cut 2 Template #3 (total of 36 triangles).

From light background, cut border strips before cutting squares:

2 strips, each 2½" x 36½", for sides;
2 strips, each 2½" x 40½", for top and bottom;
9 squares, each 4½" x 4½";
54 squares, each 2⅞" x 2⅞"; cut squares once diagonally to yield 108 half-
    square triangles **OR** cut 108 Template #3.

Directions

1. Before assembling the blocks, arrange the pieces on your design wall,
   starting with the large triangles and plain center squares. Refer to the quilt
   plan at left for color placement. Use large triangles in the same color family
   within a loop: greens, purples, and pinks. Add the small squares next.
   Place the small medium-value triangles in their proper color positions
   according to the diagram. These medium fabrics strengthen the weave
   design and also create the pinwheel centers. Fill in the rest of the quilt top
   with the small background triangles.

2. Follow the directions on page 15 for assembling the blocks. Be careful to
   keep each block in the proper sequence. Square up the sides of the blocks
   as you complete them and return them to their correct position.

3. Sew the blocks together into horizontal rows. Press the seams in opposite
   directions from row to row. Sew the rows together, making sure to match
   the seams between the blocks.

4. Sew the border strips to the sides first, then to the top and bottom edges
   of the quilt top, as shown on page 60.

5. Layer the quilt top with batting and backing; baste.

6. Quilt as desired.

7. Bind the edges of the quilt.

> **Creative Option:** Make a binding using various lengths of strips from the different fabrics of one of the colors used in the design.

Old-Fashioned Love

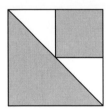

Quilt Stats

Quilt Size: 50" x 54"

Number of Blocks:
110 Shaded Four Patch

Design Layout:
Heart block repeat
Layout #27

Design Value: Dark

Theme: Hearts

Color Scheme: Scrappy
Color photo on page 26.

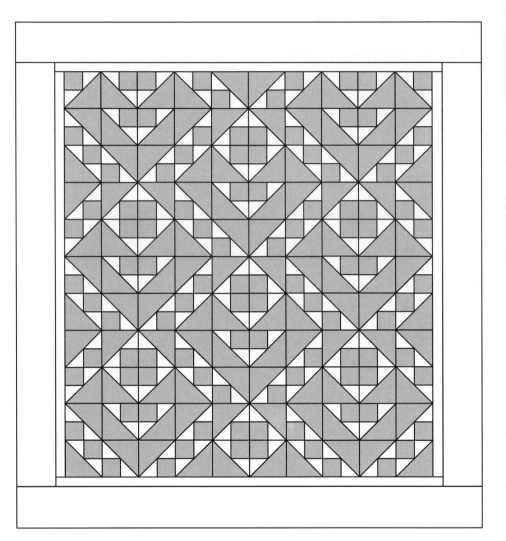

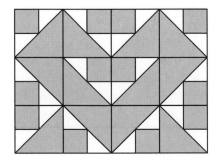

Materials: *44"-wide fabric*

Assorted dark, medium, and light fabrics for blocks
⅓ yd. for inner border
1 yd. for outer border (I used 2 different fabrics to support the scrap look.)
⅓ yd. for binding
3⅛ yds. for backing

Cutting

Follow directions on pages 13–14 for cutting triangles and squares.

From assorted darks, cut:
55 squares, each 4⅞" x 4⅞"; cut squares once diagonally to yield 110 half-square triangles **OR** cut 110 Template #1;
110 squares, each 2½" x 2½", **OR** cut 110 Template #2;

From assorted mediums and lights, cut:
110 squares, each 2⅞" x 2⅞"; cut squares once diagonally to yield 220 half-square triangles **OR** cut 220 Template #3.

From inner border fabric, cut:
6 strips, each 1¼" x 42"; join these to make one continuous strip, then cut:
    2 strips, each 44½" long, for sides;
    2 strips, each 42" long, for top and bottom.

From outer border fabric, cut:
6 strips, each 4½" x 42"; join these to make one continuous strip, then cut:
    2 strips, each 46" long, for sides;
    2 strips, each 50" long, for top and bottom.

Directions

1. Follow the general directions on page 15 for assembling the Shaded Four Patch blocks.
2. Arrange the blocks as shown in the quilt plan at left.
3. Sew the blocks together into horizontal rows. Press the seams in opposite directions from row to row. Sew the rows together, making sure to match the seams between the blocks.
4. Sew the inner border strips to the sides first, then to the top and bottom edges of the quilt top, as shown on page 60. Add the outer border strips in the same manner.
5. Layer the quilt top with batting and backing; baste.
6. Quilt as desired.
7. Bind the edges of the quilt.

Octopus's Garden

Quilt Stats

Quilt Size: 54¼" x 59½"

Number of Blocks:
92 dark Shaded Four Patch
36 light Shaded Four Patch

Design Layout:
Bar variation (blocks
set on point)
Variation of Layout #3

Design Value: Dark and light

Theme: Marine life

Color Scheme:
Blue and green with
purple accents

Color photo on page 17.

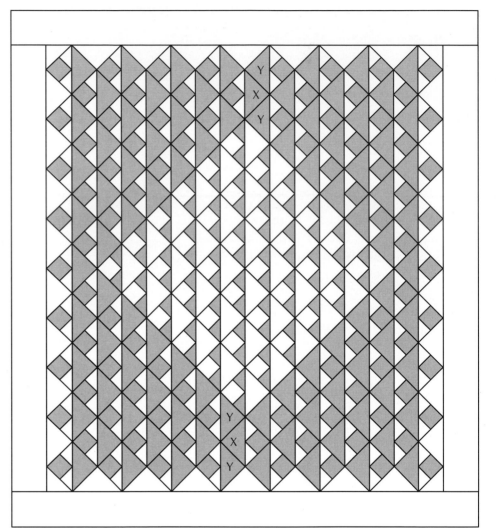

Dark

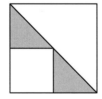

Light

Materials: *44"-wide fabric*

Select an assortment of fabrics that support the theme and/or color scheme, using a good proportion of large-scale prints to create movement and texture.

Assorted dark, medium, and light fabrics for blocks
1⅝ yds. for side and corner triangles and borders
⅓ yd. for binding
3⅓ yds. for backing

Cutting

Follow directions on pages 13–14 for cutting triangles and squares.

Center Blocks

From assorted lights and mediums, cut:
18 squares, each 4⅞" x 4⅞"; cut squares once diagonally to yield 36 half-square triangles **OR** cut 36 Template #1;
36 squares, each 2½" x 2½", **OR** cut 36 Template #2; cut 1 square to match each large triangle.

From assorted darks, cut:
36 squares, each 2⅞" x 2⅞"; cut squares once diagonally to yield 72 half-square triangles **OR** cut 72 Template #3.

Background Blocks

From assorted darks, cut:
46 squares, each 4⅞" x 4⅞"; cut squares once diagonally to yield 92 half-square triangles **OR** cut 92 Template #1;
92 squares, each 2½" x 2½", **OR** cut 92 Template #2.

From assorted mediums and lights, cut:
92 squares, each 2⅞" x 2⅞"; cut squares once diagonally to yield 184 half-square triangles **OR** cut 184 Template #3.

Borders and Setting Pieces

From the border fabric, cut border strips on the lengthwise grain before cutting remaining pieces:
4 border strips, each 4½" x 55";
1 strip, 7" x 58"; crosscut into 8 squares, each 7" x 7", then cut squares twice diagonally to yield 32 quarter-square triangles; you will use only 30 for side triangles.
2 squares, each 4" x 4"; cut squares once diagonally to yield 4 half-square triangles for corners.

Template method for cutting setting pieces:
Cut 30 Template #1, placing the long side of the triangles on the straight grain of the fabric.
Cut 4 Template #4 (page 51).

Directions

Center (Light) Blocks

1. Follow the general directions on page 15 for assembling the Shaded Four Patch blocks. For each block, use 2 small triangles from the same dark fabric, and a large triangle and small square from the same light or medium fabric.
2. Arrange the blocks on your design wall, placing them on point to form the light center square. Use clear high-contrast blocks at the outside edges of the center, particularly in the 4 corners. This creates more contrast between the center blocks and the background blocks and further emphasizes the design.

Background (Dark) Blocks

1. Assemble the background blocks in a more random manner; do not use the same fabric twice in any one block. Before assembling the background blocks, place the pieces around the center square. Begin by placing the large triangles, reversing their direction in the middle of the quilt as shown in the quilt plan on page 48.

   There are 2 areas in the design where this change in direction creates a solid line if 3 dark triangles of the same value end up next to each other. Notice the Y-X-Y triangles at the center top and center bottom of the quilt plan on page 48. You can avoid the appearance of a solid line by changing the value of the 3 triangles slightly. Place a brighter dark triangle in the X position and deeper dark triangles in the adjacent Y positions. This simple trick will break up the solid line.
2. Once the large triangles are in place, add the squares and small triangles. Use your value-determining tools to help you identify areas that need to be strengthened or toned down. Place darker, low-contrast blocks around the center square to make the center appear lighter.
3. When you are pleased with the design, assemble the blocks. It can be difficult to keep track of on-point blocks if you try to assemble too many at a time. I was able to minimize mistakes by assembling only 2 blocks at a time and returning them to the design wall. Refer to the layout often to double-check that blocks are facing the right direction.
4. On your design wall, add the side and corner triangles around the edges of the quilt. See page 58 for assembling quilts set on point. Sew the blocks together in diagonal rows. Press the seams in opposite directions from row to row. Sew the rows together, making sure to match the seams between the blocks. Add the 4 corner triangles last.
5. Some trimming and squaring up of corners may be necessary. Align the 1/4" mark on your ruler with the outside corners of the blocks. Trim the excess fabric with a rotary cutter so that a 1/4"-wide seam allowance remains.
6. Measure, trim, and sew the borders to the sides first, then to the top and bottom edges of the quilt top, as shown on page 60.
7. Layer the quilt top with batting and backing; baste.

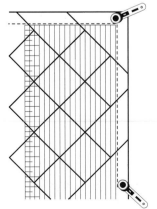

Trim the edges of the quilt to 1/4" from the block points.

8. Quilt as desired, or use the quilting design below to mark each of the
   blocks.
9. Bind the edges of the quilt.

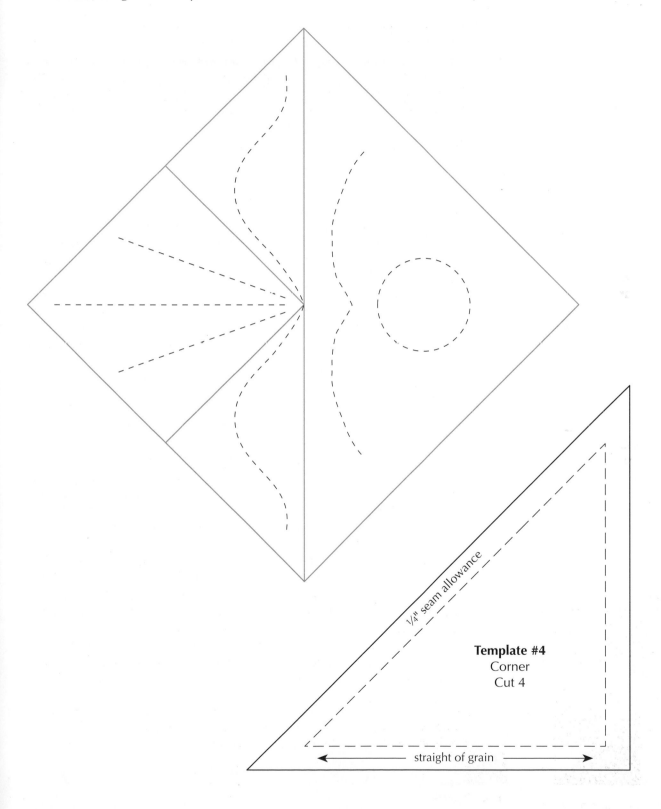

¼" seam allowance

Template #4
Corner
Cut 4

straight of grain

Tribute to Suzanne

Quilt Stats

Quilt Size: 52½" x 68½"

Number of Blocks:

70 Shaded Four Patch

36 high-contrast Four Patch

34 low-contrast Four Patch

26 dark half-square triangle border units

26 medium and light half-square triangle border units

Design Layout: Double Ladder Layout #20

Design Value: Dark

Color Scheme: Scrappy

Color photo on page 22.

High-Contrast Block

Low-Contrast Block

Light Border Block

Dark Border Block

Materials: *44"-wide fabric*

Assorted dark, medium, and light fabrics for Shaded Four Patch blocks
Assorted dark, medium dark, medium light, and clear light fabrics for Four Patch blocks
Assorted dark, medium, and light fabrics for border units
Assorted lights and mediums
1⅞ yds. for border units and border
⅜ yd. for binding
3¼ yds. for backing

Cutting

Follow directions on pages 13–14 for cutting triangles and squares.

Shaded Four Patch Blocks

From assorted darks, cut:
35 large squares, each 4⅞" x 4⅞"; cut squares once diagonally to yield 70 half-square triangles **OR** cut 70 Template #1;
70 squares, each 2½" x 2½", **OR** cut 70 Template #2.

From assorted lights and mediums, cut:
70 squares, each 2⅞" x 2⅞"; cut squares once diagonally to yield 140 half-square triangles **OR** cut 140 Template #3.

Four Patch Blocks

From assorted darks, cut:
140 squares, each 2½" x 2½", **OR** cut 140 Template #2.

From assorted medium darks, cut:
68 squares, each 2½" x 2½", for the low-contrast blocks **OR** cut 68 Template #2.

From assorted medium lights and clear lights, cut:
72 squares, each 2½" x 2½", for the high-contrast blocks **OR** cut 72 Template #2.

Border Units

From assorted darks, cut:
13 squares, each 4⅞" x 4⅞"; cut squares once diagonally to yield 26 half-square triangles **OR** cut 26 Template #1.

From assorted mediums and lights, cut:
13 squares, each 4⅞" x 4⅞"; cut squares once diagonally to yield 26 half-square triangles **OR** cut 26 Template #1.

From border fabric, cut border strips from the lengthwise grain before cutting remaining pieces:
2 strips, each 2½" x 64½", for sides;
2 strips, each 2½" x 52½", for top and bottom.
26 squares, each 4⅞" x 4⅞"; cut squares once diagonally to yield 52 half-square triangles **OR** cut 52 Template #1;

Directions

1. Follow the general directions on page 15 for assembling the Shaded Four Patch blocks.
2. Sew the dark, medium, and light squares together as shown to make the Four Patch blocks. Combine clear light and medium light squares with dark squares to make high-contrast blocks, and medium dark squares with dark squares to make low-contrast blocks.

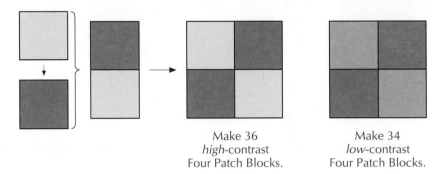

Make 36
high-contrast
Four Patch Blocks.

Make 34
low-contrast
Four Patch Blocks.

3. Sew each of the dark, medium, and light half-square triangles to a border half-square triangle to make the border blocks as shown.

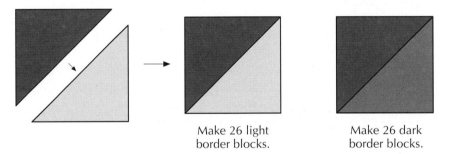

Make 26 light
border blocks.

Make 26 dark
border blocks.

4. Arrange the Shaded Four Patch blocks, Four Patch blocks, and border blocks as shown in the quilt plan on page 52. Sew the blocks together into horizontal rows. Press the seams in opposite directions from row to row. Join the rows together, making sure to match the seams between the blocks.
5. Sew border strips to the sides first, then to the top and bottom edges of the quilt top, as shown on page 60.
6. Layer the quilt top with batting and backing; baste.
7. Quilt as desired.
8. Bind the edges of the quilt.

Nicole's Star

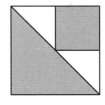
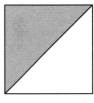

Quilt Stats

Quilt Size: 78" x 110"

Number of Blocks:
288 Shaded Four Patch
96 half-square triangle

Design Layout: Star Block repeat
Layout #30

Design Value: Dark

Theme: Stars

Color Scheme:
Black and green with red accents

Color photo on page 23.

Materials: 44"-wide fabric

½ yd. each of 6 different black fabrics
½ yd. each of 6 different dark green fabrics
⅛ yd. each of 12 different red fabrics
2¾ yds. light background
½ yd. for inner border
2 yds. for pieced outer border (2¾ yds. for unpieced border cut from lengthwise grain)
½ yd. for binding
6½ yds. for backing

Cutting

Follow directions on pages 13–14 for cutting triangles and squares.

From *each* of the 6 blacks and 6 greens, cut:

16 squares, each 4⅞" x 4⅞"; cut squares once diagonally to yield 32 half-square triangles **OR** cut 32 Template #1 (total 384 triangles)

24 squares, each 2½" x 2½", **OR** cut 24 Template #2 (total of 288 squares)

From *each* of the 12 reds, cut:

8 squares, each 2½" x 2½", **OR** cut 8 Template #2 (total of 96 squares)

From the light background, cut:

48 squares, each 4⅞" x 4⅞"; cut squares once diagonally to yield 96 half-square triangles **OR** cut 96 Template #1;

288 squares, each 2⅞" x 2⅞"; cut squares once diagonally to yield 576 half-square triangles **OR** cut 576 Template #3.

From inner border fabric, cut:

10 strips, each 1¼" x 42"; join strips to make one long continuous strip, then cut:
    2 strips, each 1¼" x 96½", for sides
    2 strips, each 1¼" x 66", for top and bottom

From outer border fabric, cut:

10 strips, each 6½" x 42"; join strips to make one long continuous strip, then cut:
    2 strips, each 6½" x 98", for sides
    2 strips, each 6½" x 78", for top and bottom

Note: For unpieced borders, cut strips from the lengthwise grain of fabric:
    2 strips, each 6½" x 98", for sides
    2 strips, each 6½" x 78", for top and bottom

Directions

Each individual star is composed of 12 Shaded Four Patch blocks with matching large triangles (either green or black), and 4 half-square triangle blocks in the opposite color (random fabrics in either green or black) in the corners.

1. Follow the general directions on page 15 for assembling the Shaded Four Patch blocks. For each star, select 12 large triangles of one green (or black) fabric. Make 4 Shaded Four Patch blocks with randomly selected red squares. Make 8 Shaded Four Patch blocks with randomly selected black (or green) squares.

2. Make 4 half-square triangle blocks with randomly selected black (or green) triangles.

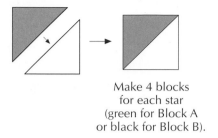

Make 4 blocks
for each star
(green for Block A
or black for Block B).

3. Assemble the blocks as shown in the piecing diagrams below to make Block A—black stars, and Block B—green stars.

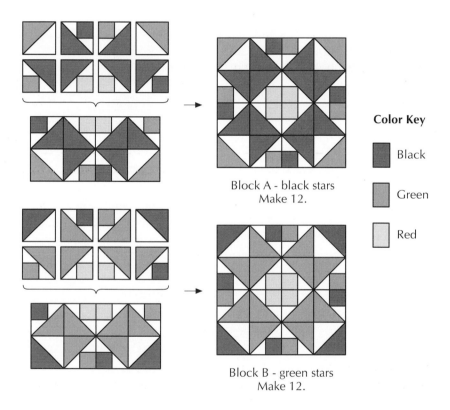

Block A - black stars
Make 12.

Color Key

▪ Black

▪ Green

▫ Red

Block B - green stars
Make 12.

4. Arrange the Star blocks in 6 rows of 4 blocks each, alternating Block A and Block B as shown in the quilt plan on page 55.
5. Sew the blocks together into horizontal rows. Press the seams in opposite directions from row to row. Join the rows together, making sure to match the seams between the blocks.
6. Sew the inner border to the sides first, then to the top and bottom edges of the quilt top as shown on page 60. Add the outer border in the same manner.
7. Layer the quilt top with batting and backing; baste.
8. Quilt as desired.
9. Bind the edges of the quilt.

General Directions

The following are general directions for assembling and finishing your quilt.

Accurate Seaming

To ensure that you are sewing accurate ¼"-wide seams, use a quilting foot (designed to measure exactly ¼" from the edge to the center needle position) or mark an accurate ¼"-wide sewing gauge on your sewing machine:

1. Place a ruler or piece of graph paper with four squares to the inch under your presser foot.
2. Lower the needle so that it pierces the paper slightly to the right of the first line on the grid. Place several layers of tape or a piece of moleskin (available in drugstores) on your throat plate along the right-hand edge of the ruler or paper, making sure it does not interfere with the feed dog. Test your new guide to make sure your seams are ¼" wide; if they are not, readjust your guide.

Chain Piecing

Chain piecing saves both time and thread.

1. Sew the first seam, but do not lift the presser foot or cut the threads.
2. Feed the next pair of pieces under the presser foot, as close as possible to the first pair, and stitch. There will be a twist of thread between the two pairs.
3. Continue sewing all the seams you can at one time, then remove the "chain."
4. Clip the threads and press the seam allowances to one side (toward the darker fabric wherever possible).

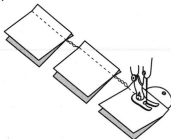

Chain sewing

Assembling the Blocks

When you are satisfied with the design layout you are ready to assemble the quilt top. For straight-set quilts, arrange blocks side by side and sew them together in horizontal or vertical rows. Press seam allowances in opposite directions from row to row. Then join the rows to complete the pattern section of the quilt.

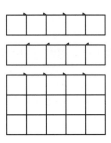

Straight-Set Quilts

For diagonally set quilts, set blocks on point. Arrange the blocks and setting triangles, following the quilt plan. Sew the blocks together into diagonal rows. Press seam allowances in opposite directions from row to row. Then join the rows together, adding the corner triangles last.

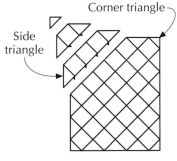

Corner triangle

Side triangle

Diagonally Set Quilts

Setting Triangles

Setting triangles are added to the sides and corners of diagonally set quilts to complete the quilt top. They can be quick-cut from squares.

Quarter-square triangles   Half-square triangles
for sides   for corners

Quarter-square triangles are used along the outside edges of the quilt because their short sides are cut on the bias and their long side on the straight grain. This keeps the edges of the quilt from stretching. Cut a square 1¼" larger than the long side of the finished triangle. Then cut the square twice diagonally to yield 4 quarter-square triangles.

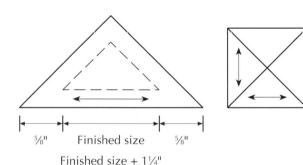

⅝"   Finished size   ⅝"

Finished size + 1¼"

Half-square triangles are used in the corners because their short sides are cut on the straight grain and their long side on the bias. This keeps the corners of the quilt from stretching. Cut a square ⅞" larger than the short sides of the finished triangle. Then cut the square once diagonally to yield two half-square triangles.

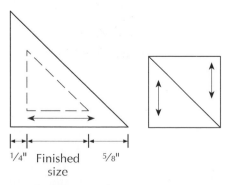

¼"   Finished   ⅝"
size

Finished size + ⅞"

If plain alternate blocks or panels are used, make them the same size as the primary blocks (including seam allowance). Arrange the primary and alternate blocks according to the design and sew them into rows. Then join the rows together.

Adding Borders

Whether or not you add a border to your quilt is entirely up to you. Some quilts do not even need a border. This section provides instructions for straight-cut borders. This type of border is much easier to piece than the mitered kind, and it also adheres to our original goal of keeping things simple.

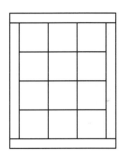

Straight-Cut Borders

Yardage requirements for most borders are based on border strips cut across the width of the fabric and pieced as necessary to make one long continuous strip. Cut border strips to the required measurements for the sides and the top and bottom as described on page 60.

If you prefer to have the seams centered on the sides of the quilt top, you will need to cut extra strips. Piece strips as necessary so that the seams are centered on the sides of the quilt top when two strips are joined, or placed equidistant from the center when three strips are joined.

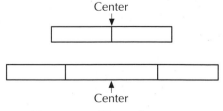

Center

Center

Measure equidistant from center.

If you prefer unpieced borders, you will have to buy more fabric and cut the border strips from the lengthwise grain of the fabric. You will have fabric left over to use in other projects.

Although the instructions for individual quilts provide measurements for cutting borders, it's a good idea to measure your finished quilt top first to make sure it fits the quilt dimensions given. If your top ends up larger or smaller, adjust the border measurements to fit your dimensions. Not everyone sews a perfect ¼" seam. As long as your piece is symmetrical, it won't matter.

Sew border strips to the left and right sides of the quilt top first, then to the top and bottom edges. This sequence—sides first, top and bottom last—helps the quilt hang straighter.

To determine the correct border measurements:

1. Measure the length of the quilt top through the center. Cut two border strips to that measurement. Mark the center point on each side of the quilt top and on the border strips. Pin the border strips to the sides of the quilt top, matching center marks and upper and lower edges. Sew the border strips in place and press seam allowances toward the border.

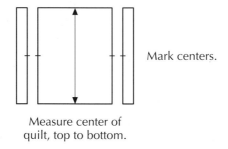

Mark centers.

Measure center of quilt, top to bottom.

2. Measure the width of the quilt through the center, including the side borders just added. Cut border strips to that measurement. Mark the center point on the top and bottom edges of the quilt top and on the border strips. Pin the border strips to the top and bottom edges, matching center marks and side edges. Sew the border strips in place and press seam allowances toward the border.

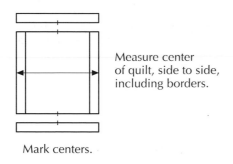

Measure center of quilt, side to side, including borders.

Mark centers.

Marking the Quilt Top

If you are planning to do straight-line or outline quilting, use masking tape to mark the quilt after it has been layered with batting and backing. Apply the tape when you are ready to quilt a line and remove it promptly after quilting. Tape left on the quilt for too long may leave a residue that is impossible to remove.

Mark more complex quilting designs on the quilt before layering the quilt with batting and backing. Work on a hard, smooth surface. Use a hard lead pencil (number 3 or 4) on light fabrics. For dark fabrics, try a fine-line chalk marker or a silver or white pencil. Light lines are always easier to remove than heavy ones: test on a scrap of fabric to make sure that whatever you use will wash out after quilting is completed.

Making the Backing

The quilt backing should extend 2" – 4" beyond the outer edges of the quilt top. A single length of fabric will be enough to back a quilt that is no wider than 38". For a larger quilt, buy extra-wide cotton or sew two or more pieces of fabric together. Use a single fabric, pieced as necessary, to make a backing of adequate size, or piece a simple multi-fabric back that complements the front of the quilt. Early quiltmakers often made multi-fabric backings as a matter of necessity; modern quiltmakers see quilt backings as another place to experiment with color and design.

If you opt for a pieced backing, trim the selvages before you sew and press seams open. Seam single-fabric backings horizontally to conserve fabric.

Choosing the Right Batting

Batting comes packaged in standard bed sizes; you can also purchase it by the yard. Several weights, or thicknesses, are available. Thick battings are fine for tied quilts and comforters. Choose a thinner batting if you intend to quilt by hand or machine.

Thin batting is available in an 80%/20% cotton/polyester blend, 100% cotton, and 100% polyester. The cotton/polyester blend supposedly combines the best features of the two fibers. All-cotton batting is soft and drapable but requires close quilting and produces quilts that are rather flat. Though many quilters like the antique look, some find cotton batting difficult to "needle." Glazed or bonded polyester batting requires less quilting and has more loft. It is sturdy, easy to work with, and washes well. However, polyester fibers sometimes migrate through fabric, creating tiny white "beards" on the surface of a quilt. The dark gray and black polyester battings now available may alleviate this problem for quiltmakers who like to work with dark fabrics—bearding will be less noticeable.

Unroll your batting and let it relax overnight before you layer your quilt. Some battings may need to be prewashed, while others definitely should not be; be sure to check the manufacturer's instructions. Cut batting 2" larger than the quilt top all the way around, or the same size as the backing.

Layering the Quilt

Once your quilt top has been marked, your backing pieced, and your batting "relaxed," you are ready to layer the quilt.

1. Spread the backing, wrong side up, on a flat, clean surface and anchor it with pins or masking tape.
2. Spread the batting over the backing, smoothing out any wrinkles.
3. Center the quilt top on the backing, face up. Be careful not to stretch or distort any of the layers as you work.
4. Starting in the middle, pin-baste the three layers together, gently smoothing any fullness to the sides and corners.
5. Baste the three layers together with a long needle and light-colored thread. Start in the center and work diagonally to each corner, making a large X. Continue basting, filling in a grid of horizontal and vertical lines 6"–8" apart. Finish by basting around the outside edges.

Quilting

The purpose of quilting is to keep the three layers together and to prevent the batting from lumping or shifting.

Traditional Hand Quilting

To quilt by hand, you will need short, sturdy needles (called "betweens"), quilting thread, and a thimble. Most quilters also use a frame or hoop to support their work. Quilting needles run from size 8 to 12: the bigger the number, the smaller the needle. Use the smallest needle you can comfortably handle; the smaller the needle is, the smaller your stitches will be.

Thread your needle with a single strand of quilting thread about 18" long. Make a small knot and insert the needle in the top layer about 1" from the place you want to start stitching. Pull the needle out at the point where the quilting will begin and gently pull the thread until the knot pops through the fabric and into the batting. Begin your quilting line with a backstitch, inserting the needle straight down through all three layers. Continue by taking small, even running stitches, rocking the needle up and down through all layers until you have three or four stitches on the needle. Place your other hand underneath the quilt so you can feel the needle point with the tip of your finger when you take a stitch. The hand underneath works in concert with the hand on top, manipulating the needle and fabric to achieve small, even stitches.

To end a line of quilting, make a small knot close to the last stitch; then, backstitch, running the thread a needle's length through the batting. Gently pull the thread until the knot pops into the batting; clip the thread next to the surface of the quilt. Remove basting stitches as you quilt, leaving only those that go around the outside edges of the quilt.

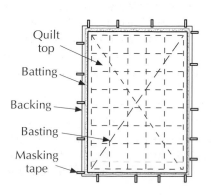

Quilt top
Batting
Backing
Basting
Masking tape

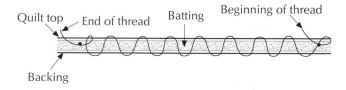

Quilt top — End of thread — Batting — Beginning of thread

Backing

Machine Quilting

Machine quilting is suitable for all types of quilts, from baby and bed quilts that will be washed frequently to glamorous pieces for the wall. With machine quilting, you can quickly complete quilts that might otherwise languish on shelves. The technique provides some creative challenges as well.

Basting for machine quilting is usually done with safety pins. If you have a large work surface to support the quilt and an even-feed (or "walking") foot for your sewing machine, you should have no problem with shifting layers or untidy pleats, tucks, and bubbles on the back side. Remove the safety pins as you sew. Pull the thread ends to the back and work them into the quilt for a professional look.

Try machine quilting with threads of unusual types and weights, or experiment with the decorative stitch or twin-needle capabilities of your sewing machine.

Marking is only necessary if you need to follow a grid or a complex pattern. It is not necessary if you plan to quilt in-the-ditch, outline quilt a uniform distance from seam lines, or free-motion quilt in a random pattern.

1. For straight-line quilting, it is extremely helpful to have a walking foot to help feed the quilt layers through the machine without shifting or puckering. Some machines have a built-in walking foot; other machines require a separate attachment.

Walking foot

Quilting-in-the-Ditch   Outline Quilting

2. For free-motion quilting, you need a darning foot and the ability to drop the feed dog on the machine. With free-motion quilting, you do not turn the fabric under the needle but instead guide the fabric in the direction of the design. Use free-motion quilting to outline a quilt pattern in the fabric or to create stippling and many other curved designs.

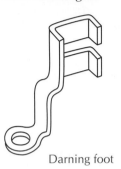

Darning foot

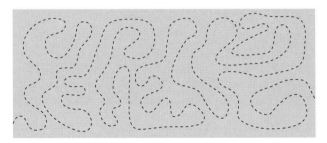

Free-Motion Quilting

Binding the Quilt

The binding should support the surface and bring your eye back to the center rather than away from it. Audition different fabrics until you achieve the proper effect.

When quilting is complete, prepare for binding by removing any remaining basting threads, except for the stitches around the outside edges of the quilt. Trim the batting and backing even with the edges of the quilt top. Use a rotary cutter and ruler to get accurate straight edges; make sure the corners are square.

Straight-grain binding is fine for most applications, but bias binding wears better.

Mitered Binding

1. For a 1/4" finished binding with mitered corners, cut 1 1/2"-wide straight-grain strips from your binding fabric.

Note: To cut bias strips, fold a square on the diagonal, then fold the resulting triangle 2 more times as shown. Cut 1½"–wide strips, perpendicular to the straight edges as shown.

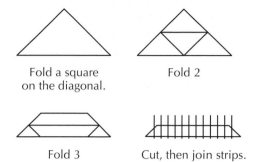

Fold a square
on the diagonal.   Fold 2

Fold 3   Cut, then join strips.

2. Trim the ends of straight-grain strips at a 45° angle. Sew strips together to make one long continuous strip. Press seam allowances open.

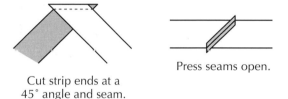

Cut strip ends at a
45° angle and seam.   Press seams open.

3. Turn under ¼" at a 45° angle at one end of the strip and press.

4. Starting 8"–10" from a corner, lay the binding on the front of the quilt, with the raw edges of the binding even with the raw edges of the quilt. Sew the binding to the quilt with a ¼"-wide seam; leave the first few inches of the binding free so that you can overlap the end of the binding with the beginning. Stop stitching ¼" from the corner of the quilt; backstitch and clip threads.

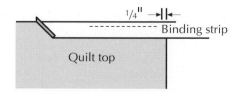

¼"
Binding strip
Quilt top

5. Turn the quilt in preparation for sewing the next edge. Fold the binding up, away from the quilt. Fold the binding back down onto itself, parallel with the edge of the quilt top. Sew from the edge to the next corner, stopping ¼" from the corner as before; backstitch and clip the threads. Fold the binding as before and continue around the edge of the quilt.

Quilt top   Quilt top

6. When you reach the starting point, overlap the beginning stitches by about 1" and cut away the excess binding, trimming the end at a 45° angle. Finish the seam.

Quilt top

7. Fold the binding over the raw edges of the quilt to the back. Turn the raw edges of the binding under ¼" and blindstitch in place, covering the machine stitching. Make sure the stitches do not go through to the front of the quilt. Fold the binding at the corners to form miters on the front and back of the quilt. Stitch to secure.

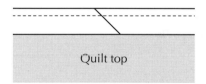

Quilt back   Quilt back

**Layout 1
Ladder - single**

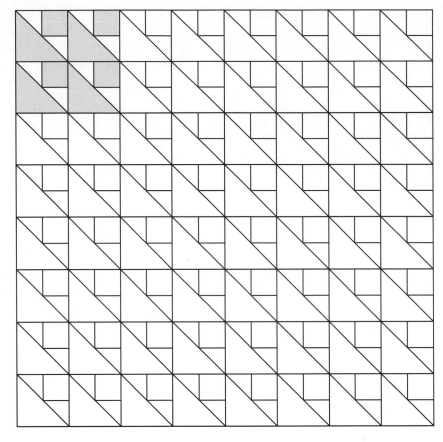

**Layout 2
Ladder - double**

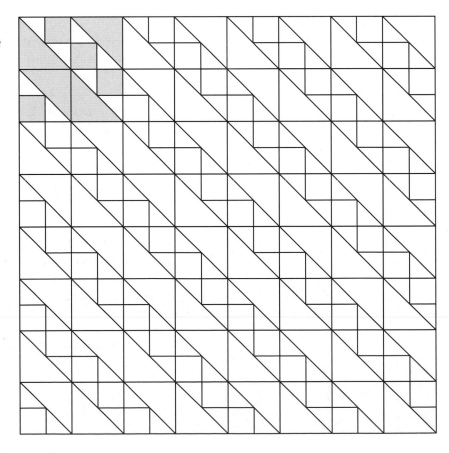

**Layout 3
Bar - single**

**Layout 4
Bar - double**

Layout 5
Chevron - single

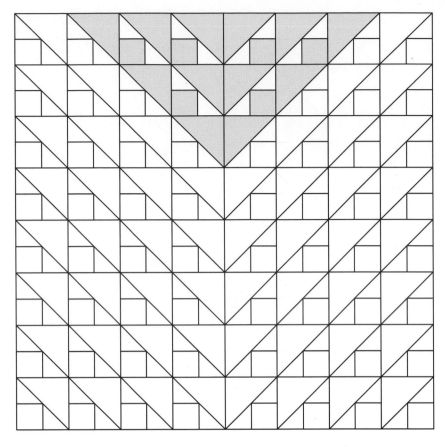

Layout 6
Chevron - double

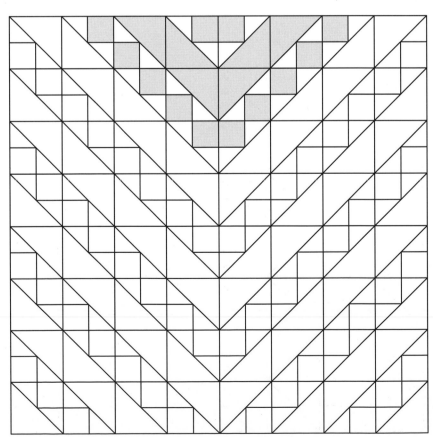

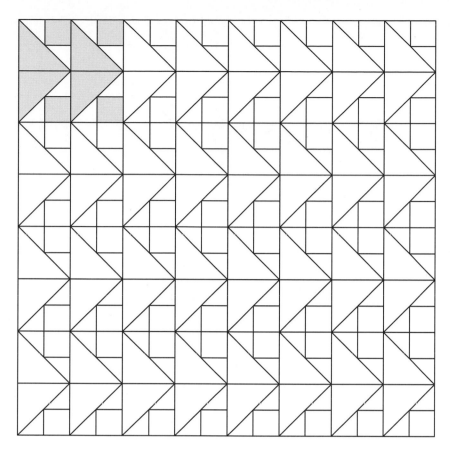

**Layout 7
Zigzag - single**

**Layout 8
Zigzag - double**

**Layout 9
X - single**

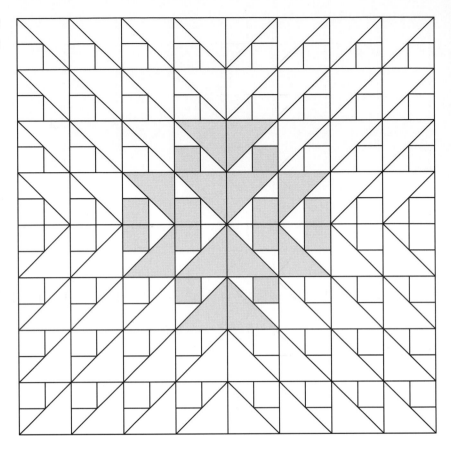

**Layout 10
X - double**

**Layout 11
X - double variation**

**Layout 12
Combination - Barn
Raising Center, X, and
Chevron background**

**Layout 13
Barn Raising - single**

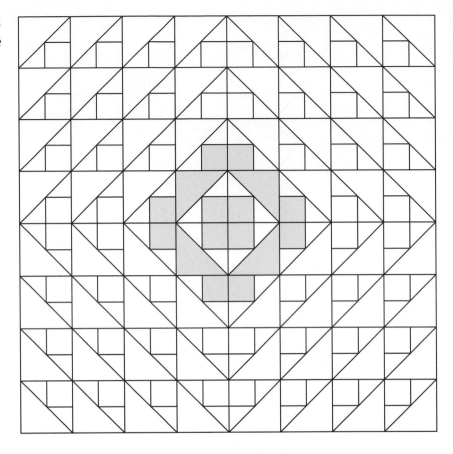

**Layout 14
Barn Raising - double**

**Layout 15
Squares and
Circles - double**

**Layout 16
Mini Barn
Raising**

**Layout 17
Squares and
Circles - squared**

**Layout 18
Weave**

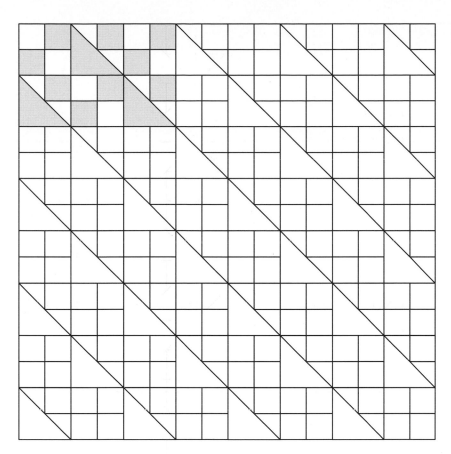

Layout 19
Ladder/Four Patch - single

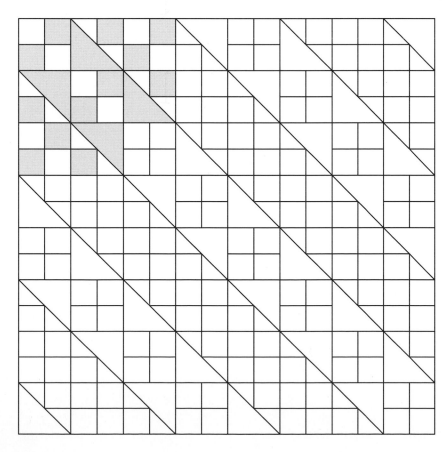

Layout 20
Ladder/Four Patch - double

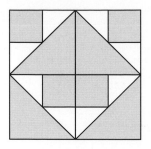

Layout 21
Arrow

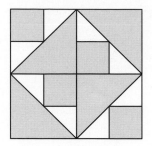

Layout 22
Lantern

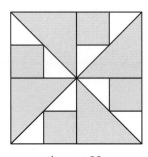

Layout 23
Pinwheel

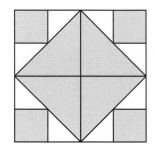

Layout 24
Box

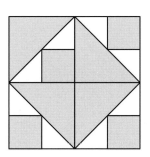

Layout 25
Tulip

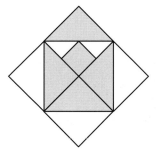

Layout 26
Envelope*

Design contributed by Mary Ann Hatfield.

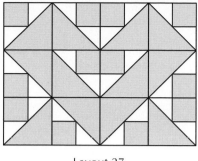

Layout 27
Heart

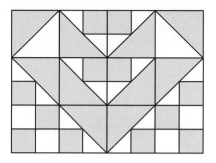

Layout 28
Flower*

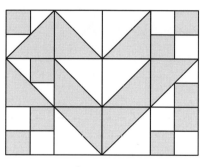

Layout 29
Bird*

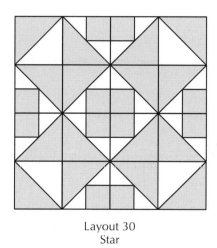

Layout 30
Star

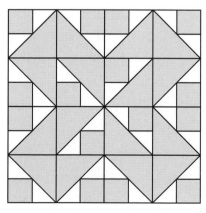

Layout 31
Double Z's

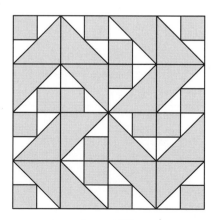

Layout 32
Whirlygig

Design contributed by Marilyn Anderson.

Fabric Sources

Catalogs are available from the following:

FL-AIR

Airbrush Fabric Design
487 A Hwy 9
Sedro-Wooley, WA 98284
(206) 856-4988

Intercontinental Business Network

PO Box 616 Rockefeller Center Station
New York, NY 10185
Attn: Homeland Fashions Dept.
1-800-AFRICAN
Swatch book of African fabric samples

International Fabric Collection

5152 Wolf Road
Erie, PA 16505
1-800-462-3891
Japanese, African, and other ethnic fabrics

Kasuri Dyeworks

1959 Shattuck Ave.
Berkeley, CA 94704
(415) 841-4509
Japanese fabrics

Suzanne Tessier Hammond has been making quilts for more than 20 years. She received her sewing experience making garments first for herself, then for others, and finally for specialty shops near Buffalo, New York, all the while making simple quilts for family and friends from the leftovers. When the rest of the world rediscovered quiltmaking, she took advantage of the many quilt classes and seminars to extend her skills and began teaching her own classes in 1985. Today, her lectures and workshops focus on quilt designing. Her quilts have been exhibited in both local and national shows and have won numerous ribbons and awards, including an award for outstanding quilting.

As a founding member of Evergreen Quilters Guild (1982), Northwest Quilting Connection (1984), and more recently, a contemporary quilt group, Quilters on the Edge (1990), she has been helpful in getting quilters united. She also is an active member of Quilters Anonymous and the American Quilting Association.

Suzanne has introduced quilting to the younger generation by providing programs for elementary and middle schools on both quilting in history and quilting as art. "Being the mother of three girls, I felt it was important that my daughters not see my work as 'women's work'. I wanted them to learn to value quilts as art rather than just piecing scraps of fabric together. Educating their classmates was part of the deal."

Her other interests include gardening and collecting frog paraphernalia. Suzanne frequently signs her pieces by quilting her frog logo somewhere on the quilt surface.

That Patchwork Place Publications and Products

BOOKS

All the Blocks Are Geese by Mary Sue Suit
Angle Antics by Mary Hickey
Animas Quilts by Jackie Robinson
Appliqué Borders: An Added Grace by Jeana Kimball
Appliquilt: Whimsical One-Step Appliqué by Tonee White
Baltimore Bouquets by Mimi Dietrich
Basket Garden by Mary Hickey
Biblical Blocks by Rosemary Makhan
Blockbuster Quilts by Margaret J. Miller
Botanical Wreaths by Laura M. Reinstatler
Calendar Quilts by Joan Hanson
Cathedral Window: A Fresh Look by Nancy J. Martin
The Cat's Meow by Janet Kime
Colourwash Quilts by Deirdre Amsden
Corners in the Cabin by Paulette Peters
Country Medallion Sampler by Carol Doak
Country Threads by Connie Tesene and Mary Tendall
Easy Machine Paper Piecing by Carol Doak
Easy Quilts...By Jupiter!® by Mary Beth Maison
Even More by Trudie Hughes
Fantasy Flowers by Doreen Cronkite Burbank
Fit To Be Tied by Judy Hopkins
Five- and Seven-Patch Blocks & Quilts for the ScrapSaver by Judy Hopkins
Four-Patch Blocks & Quilts for the ScrapSaver by Judy Hopkins
Fun with Fat Quarters by Nancy J. Martin
Go Wild with Quilts by Margaret Rolfe
Handmade Quilts by Mimi Dietrich
Happy Endings by Mimi Dietrich
Holiday Happenings by Christal Carter
Home for Christmas by Nancy J. Martin and Sharon Stanley
In The Beginning by Sharon Evans Yenter
Irma's Sampler by Irma Eskes
Jacket Jazz by Judy Murrah
Lessons in Machine Piecing by Marsha McCloskey
Little By Little: Quilts in Miniature by Mary Hickey
Little Quilts by Alice Berg, Sylvia Johnson, and Mary Ellen Von Holt
Lively Little Logs by Donna McConnell
Loving Stitches by Jeana Kimball
Make Room for Quilts by Nancy J. Martin
More Template-Free® Quiltmaking by Trudie Hughes
Nifty Ninepatches by Carolann M. Palmer
Nine-Patch Blocks & Quilts for the ScrapSaver by Judy Hopkins
Not Just Quilts by Jo Parrott
Oh! Christmas Trees compiled by Barbara Weiland

On to Square Two by Marsha McCloskey
Osage County Quilt Factory by Virginia Robertson
Painless Borders by Sally Schneider
A Perfect Match by Donna Lynn Thomas
Picture Perfect Patchwork by Naomi Norman
Piecemakers® Country Store by the Piecemakers
Pineapple Passion by Nancy Smith and Lynda Milligan
A Pioneer Doll and Her Quilts by Mary Hickey
Pioneer Storybook Quilts by Mary Hickey
Prairie People—Cloth Dolls to Make and Cherish by Marji Hadley and J. Dianne Ridgley
Quick & Easy Quiltmaking by Mary Hickey, Nancy J. Martin, Marsha McCloskey and Sara Nephew
Quilted for Christmas compiled by Ursula Reikes
The Quilters' Companion compiled by That Patchwork Place
The Quilting Bee by Jackie Wolff and Lori Aluna
Quilts for All Seasons by Christal Carter
Quilts for Baby: Easy as A, B, C by Ursula Reikes
Quilts for Kids by Carolann M. Palmer
Quilts from Nature by Joan Colvin
Quilts to Share by Janet Kime
Red and Green: An Appliqué Tradition by Jeana Kimball
Red Wagon Originals by Gerry Kimmel and Linda Brannock
Rotary Riot by Judy Hopkins and Nancy J. Martin
Rotary Roundup by Judy Hopkins and Nancy J. Martin
Round About Quilts by J. Michelle Watts
Samplings from the Sea by Rosemary Makhan
Scrap Happy by Sally Schneider
ScrapMania by Sally Schneider
Sensational Settings by Joan Hanson
Sewing on the Line by Lesly-Claire Greenberg
Shortcuts: A Concise Guide to Rotary Cutting by Donna Lynn Thomas (metric version available)
Shortcuts Sampler by Roxanne Carter
Shortcuts to the Top by Donna Lynn Thomas
Small Talk by Donna Lynn Thomas
Smoothstitch™ Quilts by Roxi Eppler
The Stitchin' Post by Jean Wells and Lawry Thorn
Strips That Sizzle by Margaret J. Miller
Sunbonnet Sue All Through the Year by Sue Linker
Tea Party Time by Nancy J. Martin
Template-Free® Quiltmaking by Trudie Hughes
Template-Free® Quilts and Borders by Trudie Hughes
Template-Free® Stars by Jo Parrott
Watercolor Quilts by Pat Magaret and Donna Slusser
Women and Their Quilts by Nancyann Johanson Twelker

TOOLS

4" Baby Bias Square® BiRangle™ Ruby Beholder™
6" Bias Square® Pineapple Rule ScrapMaster
8" Bias Square® Rotary Mate™
Metric Bias Square® Rotary Rule™

VIDEO

Shortcuts to America's Best-Loved Quilts

Many titles are available at your local quilt shop. For more information, send $2 for a color catalog to That Patchwork Place, Inc., PO Box 118, Bothell WA 98041-0118 USA.

☎ Call 1-800-426-3126 for the name and location of the quilt shop nearest you.